DIVINE MOMENTS FOR LEADERS

Everyday Inspiration from God's Word

DIVINE MOMENTS *for* LEADERS

Everyday Inspiration from God's Word

Tyndale House Publishers, Inc.

Carol Stream, Illinois

Visit Tyndale's exciting Web site at www.tyndale.com

TYNDALE, New Living Translation, NLT, and the New Living Translation logo are
registered trademarks of Tyndale House Publishers, Inc.

Divine Moments for Leaders: Everyday Inspiration from God's Word

Managing editors: Ronald A. Beers and Amy E. Mason

Contributing writers: V. Gilbert Beers, Rebecca J. Beers, Brian R. Coffey,
Jonathan Farrar, Jeffrey Frasier, Jonathan Gray, Shawn A. Harrison, Sandy Hull,
Rhonda K. O'Brien, Douglas J. Rumford, Linda Taylor

Designed by Julie Chen

Edited by Michal Needham

ISBN-13: 978-1-4143-1229-3

ISBN-10: 1-4143-1229-6

Printed in the United States of America

14   13   12   11   10   09   08

7   6   5   4   3   2   1

Introduction

The goal of *Divine Moments for Leaders* is to help you experience a breakthrough with God, to show you how and where God is at work in your life to get your attention each day. If the Bible is really a blueprint for living, then God, through his Word, should be able to respond to any question you have for him. And he does! As you read the questions and Scripture in this book, it is amazing to see how God's answers to your daily needs are so clear and help you see with "spiritual eyes" how he is trying to break through to you. Sometimes God seems so big and mysterious that you may wonder whether he would truly bother with you. But he loves you personally and is trying to get your attention every day. This little book can help you notice the divine moments when he is trying to show you how much he cares. You can read straight through the book, or you can use it topically when you are looking for God's help in a certain area of life or if you just need more clarity about what God might say about something that is important to you. We pray this little book will be meaningful to you and help you experience many divine moments with God.

—*The editors*

Abilities

Do I have the abilities that I need to lead?

A MOMENT *with* GOD

Moses pleaded with the LORD, "O Lord, I'm not very good with words. I never have been, and I'm not now, even though you have spoken to me. I get tongue-tied, and my words get tangled." Then the LORD asked Moses, "Who makes a person's mouth? Who decides whether people speak or do not speak, hear or do not hear, see or do not see? Is it not I, the LORD? Now go! I will be with you as you speak, and I will instruct you in what to say."   EXODUS 4:10-12

Now, dear brothers and sisters, regarding your question about the special abilities the Spirit gives us. . . . There are different kinds of spiritual gifts. . . . God works in different ways. . . . A spiritual gift is given to each of us so we can help each other. . . . It is the one and only Spirit who distributes all these gifts. He alone decides which gift each person should have. . . . But our bodies have many parts, and God has put each part just where he wants it. . . . In fact, some parts of the body that seem weakest and least important are actually the most necessary. . . . All of you together are Christ's body, and each of you is a part of it.   1 CORINTHIANS 12:1, 4, 6-7, 11, 18, 22, 27

Deep within the human spirit lie a longing and a capacity to do significant things. Because you are made in the image of God, you inherited from him the desire to create, to accomplish, to make things happen. God wouldn't give you these desires without the ability to carry them out. These abilities are gifts from God to help you accomplish great things for him and to live a fulfilling life. How you use or misuse them ultimately determines your quality of life—not defined by comfort or the accumulation of wealth, but by strong character, joy, and lasting satisfaction. Your goal is to discover your abilities, develop them, and channel them toward what will achieve the greatest good for the people you lead. When God asks you to accomplish something, he gives you the resources to get the job done. Therefore, if God has put you in a position of leadership, he has given you the abilities you need.

DIVINE PROMISE

GOD HAS GIVEN US DIFFERENT GIFTS FOR DOING CERTAIN THINGS WELL.   *Romans 12:6*

Accountability

MY QUESTION *for* GOD

How can accountability help me avoid foolish mistakes?

A Moment *with* God

"You are a witness to your own decision," Joshua said.
"You have chosen to serve the Lord." "Yes," they
replied, "we are witnesses to what we have said."

Joshua 24:22

Fools think their own way is right, but the wise listen
to others.   Proverbs 12:15

If another believer is overcome by some sin, you who
are godly should gently and humbly help that person
back onto the right path. And be careful not to fall
into the same temptation yourself. Share each other's
burdens.   Galatians 6:1-2

*Y*ou may have some dark corners in your life—secret habits and private thoughts that you don't want
anyone to know about. If those hidden places were
exposed in the spotlight of God's truth, you would
have to deal with them, even give them up. Accountability is answering to someone who asks you to give
an account of your words, actions, and motives—even
those you keep in the darkest corners. Accountability
can be painful at the time, but the lack of it will destroy you in the long run. Your secret sins will eat away
at your character and integrity until your reputation
crashes down around you. Without accountability, you
wouldn't even see it coming. Determine now to find a
wise friend or mentor to keep you accountable. Don't
let the darkness take over your heart.

DIVINE PROMISE

TWO PEOPLE ARE BETTER OFF THAN ONE,
FOR THEY CAN HELP EACH OTHER SUCCEED.
IF ONE PERSON FALLS, THE OTHER CAN
REACH OUT AND HELP.   *Ecclesiastes 4:9-10*

Actions

MY QUESTION *for* GOD

*How can I value someone as a person but at the same time
correct sinful actions?*

A MOMENT *with* GOD

Everyone who sins is breaking God's law, for all sin is
contrary to the law of God.   1 JOHN 3:4

Don't just pretend to love others. Really love them.
Hate what is wrong. Hold tightly to what is good.

ROMANS 12:9

The saying "Hate the sin but love the sinner" is an effective principle to follow. When you truly love someone, you want what is best for them, and sin is never
best for anyone.

You must warn each other every day, while it is still
"today," so that none of you will be deceived by sin
and hardened against God. For if we are faithful to
the end, trusting God just as firmly as when we first
believed, we will share in all that belongs to Christ.
Remember what it says: "Today when you hear his

voice, don't harden your hearts as Israel did when
they rebelled." HEBREWS 3:13-15

First be concerned about the spiritual well-being of
others before you warn them about the consequences
of their actions. Be more concerned about restoration
than punishment.

He must have a strong belief in the trustworthy
message he was taught; then he will be able to
encourage others with wholesome teaching and show
those who oppose it where they are wrong. TITUS 1:9

Encouragement is essential in helping others change
their course of action.

[Paul said,] "I used to believe that I ought to do
everything I could to oppose the very name of Jesus
the Nazarene. . . . One day I was on such a mission to
Damascus, armed with the authority and commission
of the leading priests. About noon . . . a light from
heaven brighter than the sun shone down on me
and my companions. We all fell down, and I heard
a voice saying to me in Aramaic, 'Saul, Saul, why
are you persecuting me? . . . I am Jesus, the one you
are persecuting. Now get to your feet! For I have
appeared to you to appoint you as my servant and
witness. . . . Yes, I am sending you to the Gentiles
to open their eyes, so they may turn from darkness
to light and from the power of Satan to God."

ACTS 26:9, 12-18

*M*ake sure you are correctly assessing the situation. ·The apostle Paul (whose name was Saul before he was converted) was convinced that he was doing the right thing for God by persecuting Christians, that those he was confronting were wrong. But when he met Jesus, he realized he was wrong and had to make a major adjustment in his own convictions and actions.

DIVINE PROMISE

THE LORD OUR GOD IS MERCIFUL AND FORGIVING, EVEN THOUGH WE HAVE REBELLED AGAINST HIM.   *Daniel 9:9*

Administration

MY QUESTION *for* GOD

How does administration benefit leaders and those they lead?

A MOMENT *with* GOD

God blessed them and said, "Be fruitful and multiply. Fill the earth and govern it. Reign over the fish in the sea, the birds in the sky, and all the animals that scurry along the ground."   GENESIS 1:28

The LORD God placed the man in the Garden of Eden to tend and watch over it.   GENESIS 2:15

God said to Noah, . . . "Enter the boat—you and your wife and your sons and their wives. Bring a pair

of every kind of animal—a male and a female—
into the boat with you to keep them alive during the
flood. Pairs of every kind of bird, and every kind of
animal, and every kind of small animal that scurries
along the ground, will come to you to be kept alive.
And be sure to take on board enough food for your
family and for all the animals."   GENESIS 6:13, 18-21

Pharaoh said to Joseph, "Since God has revealed the
meaning of the dreams to you, clearly no one else is
as intelligent or wise as you are. You will be in charge
of my court, and all my people will take orders from
you. Only I, sitting on my throne, will have a rank
higher than yours."   GENESIS 41:39-40

In the Garden of Eden, God charged human beings
with the work of tending and managing his creation
so that the earth would be fruitful. In the same way,
leaders are to care for the situations and people in their
charge, working toward an environment where people
can reach their full potential. Administration is the
God-ordained task of managing time and resources in
order to accomplish that goal.

Scripture shows that God works in orderly ways to
take care of his people. Noah obeyed God's commands,
and his administrative skills saved himself, his family,
and every animal species from the Flood. God used
Joseph to manage the nation of Egypt so that the bum-
per crops of the good years would be stored and then
distributed to the hungry during the years of famine.
Leaders offer everyone a divine moment when they use

their God-given skills of administration to complete
the tasks before them.

DIVINE CHALLENGE

ALL OF YOU TOGETHER ARE CHRIST'S BODY,
AND EACH OF YOU IS A PART OF IT. . . . SO
YOU SHOULD EARNESTLY DESIRE THE MOST
HELPFUL GIFTS.   *1 Corinthians 12:27, 31*

Adversity

MY QUESTION *for* GOD

*How can I prepare for the inevitable troubles that come
my way?*

A MOMENT *with* GOD

Be truly glad. There is wonderful joy ahead, even
though you have to endure many trials for a little
while. These trials will show that your faith is
genuine. It is being tested as fire tests and purifies
gold—though your faith is far more precious than
mere gold. So when your faith remains strong
through many trials, it will bring you much praise
and glory and honor on the day when Jesus Christ is
revealed to the whole world.   1 PETER 1:6-7

I cried out to the LORD in my great trouble, and he
answered me. I called to you from the land of the
dead, and LORD, you heard me!   JONAH 2:2

In my distress I cried out to the LORD; yes, I prayed
to my God for help. He heard me from his sanctuary;
my cry to him reached his ears.   PSALM 18:6

[Jesus said,] "I have told you all this so that you may
have peace in me. Here on earth you will have many
trials and sorrows. But take heart, because I have
overcome the world."   JOHN 16:33

Athletic coaches are fond of motivational sayings
like "No pain, no gain!" or "Growth comes through
adversity." What coaches recognize is that the trials in
our lives do not have to defeat us but rather can make
us stronger if we have the proper perspective. Trouble
comes in a multitude of ways—accidents, afflictions,
calamities, difficulties, disappointments, failures,
grief, hard times, hurts, misfortunes, sufferings, trials,
woes. For leaders, there is the double burden of adversity affecting them as well as those they lead. The word
adversity means that something is acting against you.
Nowhere is this concept more clearly presented than in
the Bible, which makes it clear that God himself sometimes sends us adversity either as a punishment for sin
or simply as a way to test and strengthen our character.
Other times Satan sends adversity to try to get us to
sin, and God allows it. Sometimes we bring adversity
on ourselves by acting foolishly or sinfully. And there
is the adversity that comes from the poor decisions or
sins of others. The one thing you can count on is that
adversity will come. As a leader, you must learn to deal
with it personally and help others deal with it. Avoiding

adversity may not always be best for you or those you lead. Though it may not feel good, if you don't let it defeat you, it will in fact make you stronger. Remember that God not only listens to us during times of adversity but he is with us through them.

DIVINE PROMISE

WHEN YOU GO THROUGH DEEP WATERS, I WILL BE WITH YOU. WHEN YOU GO THROUGH RIVERS OF DIFFICULTY, YOU WILL NOT DROWN. WHEN YOU WALK THROUGH THE FIRE OF OPPRESSION, YOU WILL NOT BE BURNED UP; THE FLAMES WILL NOT CONSUME YOU.   *Isaiah 43:2*

Advice

MY QUESTION *for* GOD

How do I make sure that I am giving good advice?

A MOMENT *with* GOD

While at Micah's house, they recognized the young Levite's accent, so they went over and asked him, "Who brought you here, and what are you doing in this place? Why are you here?" He told them about his agreement with Micah and that he had been hired as Micah's personal priest. Then [the warriors] said, "Ask God whether or not our journey will be successful." "Go in peace," the priest replied. "For the LORD is watching over your journey."   JUDGES 18:3-6

The warriors in this Bible passage asked Micah's priest for godly advice. But they were asking the wrong person, for this "man of God" wasn't close to God at all. In fact, everyone in this story was out of touch with God. Godly people don't always tell us what we want to hear because sometimes they must use God's Word to convict us of our sins. Micah's priest didn't even consult God before telling the men exactly what they wanted to hear. This was spiritual arrogance and a sign that he really didn't serve God at all. A religious title doesn't necessarily make someone a godly person. The New Testament encourages us to beware of false teachers who "are hypocrites and liars, and their consciences are dead" (1 Timothy 4:2). What a fitting picture of Micah's priest. The New Testament also says we should "teach the truth so that your teaching can't be criticized" (Titus 2:8). We must "promote the kind of living that reflects wholesome teaching" and "be worthy of respect" (Titus 2:1-2). Look for these godly qualities in others before you ask them for advice. As a leader, also strive to have these qualities so that your advice will be wise.

DIVINE PROMISE

WISE WORDS ARE LIKE DEEP WATERS;
WISDOM FLOWS FROM THE WISE LIKE A
BUBBLING BROOK. *Proverbs 18:4*

Aggravation

MY QUESTION *for* GOD

How should I respond to aggravation?

A MOMENT *with* GOD

Love is patient and kind. Love is not jealous or boastful or proud or rude. It does not demand its own way. It is not irritable, and it keeps no record of being wronged.   1 CORINTHIANS 13:4-5

A peaceful heart leads to a healthy body; jealousy is like cancer in the bones.   PROVERBS 14:30

When you feel aggravated, take a step back to relax and respond in love. Determine what is causing your reaction and whether the situation really warrants the turmoil it's causing. Aggravation often feeds on itself—the more you're aggravated, the more you aggravate others.

He did not retaliate when he was insulted, nor threaten revenge when he suffered. He left his case in the hands of God who always judges fairly.   1 PETER 2:23

Don't retaliate, which often begins a negative cycle in which each person feels the need to strike back harder. In many cases, the only thing you can do is release the situation to God and wait for him to act on your behalf.

Don't sin by letting anger control you. Think about it overnight and remain silent.   Psalm 4:4

My dear brothers and sisters: You must all be quick to listen, slow to speak, and slow to get angry.   James 1:19

Slow down and carefully think through how you can respond, without sinning, to the people or situations that aggravate you. This keeps you from saying something you may later regret.

People with understanding control their anger; a hot temper shows great foolishness.   Proverbs 14:29

Control your temper, for anger labels you a fool.

Ecclesiastes 7:9

"Don't sin by letting anger control you." Don't let the sun go down while you are still angry, for anger gives a foothold to the devil.   Ephesians 4:26-27

Avoid any reaction based on anger. Anger is like a forest fire—it quickly destroys that which took a long time to grow.

DIVINE PROMISE

SENSIBLE PEOPLE CONTROL THEIR TEMPER;
THEY EARN RESPECT BY OVERLOOKING
WRONGS. *Proverbs 19:11*

Agreement

MY QUESTION for GOD

How can I reach an agreement with others without compromising my convictions?

A MOMENT with GOD

Daniel was determined not to defile himself by eating the food. . . . He asked . . . permission not to eat these unacceptable foods. . . . "Please test us for ten days on a diet of vegetables and water," Daniel said. . . . The attendant agreed to Daniel's suggestion. . . . At the end of the ten days, Daniel . . . looked healthier and better nourished than the young men who had been eating the food assigned by the king.

DANIEL 1:8, 12, 14-15

When trying to reach an agreement, there is a time to compromise and a time to stand firm. When the forces of evil want their way, you cannot budge. To compromise God's truth, God's ways, or God's Word is to negotiate with that which is unholy. The test of acceptable compromise is simple: Can both parties reach a satisfactory agreement without anyone's morals being sacrificed? To give up godliness for something less is a bad bargain. Work for harmony and agreement whenever it is possible, but when it is not, pray that God would break through the stalemate and make his will clear.

DIVINE CHALLENGE

BE ON GUARD. STAND FIRM IN THE FAITH. BE COURAGEOUS. BE STRONG.   *1 Corinthians 16:13*

Ambiguity

MY QUESTION *for* GOD

How do I deal with all the ambiguities of faith in God?

A MOMENT *with* GOD

How great is our Lord! His power is absolute! His understanding is beyond comprehension!   PSALM 147:5

Can you solve the mysteries of God? Can you discover everything about the Almighty?   JOB 11:7

Who is able to advise the Spirit of the LORD? Who knows enough to give him advice or teach him?

ISAIAH 40:13

*Y*ou can be sure that God's character is not ambiguous—he always acts justly and consistently. But God's ways may be unpredictable and mysterious. His plans sometimes surprise us and defy human logic. The inexplicable aspects of God teach us to respect him and show him the reverence he deserves. Would you want a God you could fully comprehend? Such a god would have to be an equal, not an almighty, divine being.

Jesus replied, "I tell you the truth, unless you are born again, you cannot see the Kingdom of God."

"What do you mean?" exclaimed Nicodemus. "How can an old man go back into his mother's womb and be born again?" Jesus replied, "I assure you, no one can enter the Kingdom of God without being born of water and the Spirit. Humans can reproduce only human life, but the Holy Spirit gives birth to spiritual life. So don't be surprised when I say, 'You must be born again.' The wind blows wherever it wants. Just as you can hear the wind but can't tell where it comes from or where it is going, so you can't explain how people are born of the Spirit."   JOHN 3:3-8

The message of the cross is foolish to those who are headed for destruction! But we who are being saved know it is the very power of God.   1 CORINTHIANS 1:18

Just as you don't have to fully understand electricity to enjoy light, you don't have to fully understand being born again to experience God's salvation. Faith means flipping on the switch and walking in the light.

It was to us that God revealed these things by his Spirit. For his Spirit searches out everything and shows us God's deep secrets. No one can know a person's thoughts except that person's own spirit, and no one can know God's thoughts except God's own Spirit. And we have received God's Spirit (not the world's spirit), so we can know the wonderful things God has freely given us.   1 CORINTHIANS 2:10-12

*T*he Christian life is the process of continually learning spiritual truths about God as his Spirit reveals them. Learning to recognize the voice of God's Spirit and moving where he leads are key in regularly experiencing divine moments in your life.

O LORD my God, my Holy One, you who are eternal—surely you do not plan to wipe us out? O LORD, our Rock, you have sent these Babylonians to correct us, to punish us for our many sins. But you are pure and cannot stand the sight of evil. Will you wink at their treachery? Should you be silent while the wicked swallow up people more righteous than they?   HABAKKUK 1:12-13

*H*abakkuk had questions and doubts about God's actions, but not about who he is—faithful and eternal. We can know that God is loving and just even when we do not understand why he allows some things to happen.

Now we see things imperfectly as in a cloudy mirror, but then we will see everything with perfect clarity. All that I know now is partial and incomplete, but then I will know everything completely, just as God now knows me completely.   1 CORINTHIANS 13:12

*T*he best way to view the ambiguities of faith while we live on this earth is through spiritual eyes. Knowing that things will one day be clear keeps your eyes focused on what is ultimately important.

DIVINE PROMISE
THE LORD DIRECTS OUR STEPS, SO WHY TRY TO UNDERSTAND EVERYTHING ALONG THE WAY?
Proverbs 20:24

Ambition

MY QUESTION *for* GOD

When is ambition dangerous?

A MOMENT *with* GOD

The devil took him to the peak of a very high mountain and showed him the kingdoms of the world and all their glory. "I will give it all to you," he said, "if you will kneel down and worship me." "Get out of here, Satan," Jesus told him. "For the Scriptures say, 'You must worship the LORD your God and serve only him.'"   MATTHEW 4:8-10

There's a difference between wanting to be a part of God's great work and wanting personal greatness through God's work. It's the difference between desiring to serve God and trying to use God to serve yourself. We can learn from the fact that Satan believed he could tempt Jesus by appealing to his sense of ambition. How many people have sold their souls to the devil in an attempt to gain worldly glory? When left unchecked, selfish ambition becomes the hook Satan uses to catch us and reel us in. If Jesus had been motivated by selfish ambition rather than the will and Word of God, he would have been vulnerable to the temptation to possess the kingdoms and splendor of the world. If you made a list of your five primary ambitions, what would they be? If others were to list what they believe are your five main ambitions, would they match your list? Ambition can become destructive if Satan uses it to lure you away from God. You can test your ambitions by asking yourself if they lead you closer to or farther away from God. If you're not sure about one, then it is leading you away from him. Ambition can fool you into striving after everything you desire in this world at the cost of everything God desires for you in the next.

DIVINE PROMISE

WHEN YOU FOLLOW THE DESIRES OF YOUR SINFUL NATURE, THE RESULTS ARE VERY CLEAR: . . . HOSTILITY, QUARRELING, JEALOUSY, OUTBURSTS OF ANGER, SELFISH AMBITION, DISSENSION, DIVISION, ENVY . . . AND OTHER SINS LIKE THESE. . . . BUT THE HOLY SPIRIT PRODUCES THIS KIND OF FRUIT IN OUR LIVES: LOVE, JOY, PEACE, PATIENCE, KINDNESS, GOODNESS, FAITHFULNESS, GENTLENESS, AND SELF-CONTROL.   *Galatians 5:19-23*

Ambition

MY QUESTION *for* GOD

What kind of ambition does God want me to have?

A MOMENT *with* GOD

The one thing I ask of the LORD—the thing I seek most—is to live in the house of the LORD all the days

of my life, delighting in the LORD's perfections and
meditating in his Temple.   PSALM 27:4

*H*aving a strong, vital relationship with God should
be your highest ambition. It is the one thing that can
be pursued without reservation.

God blesses those who hunger and thirst for justice,
for they will be satisfied. . . . God blesses those who
work for peace, for they will be called the children
of God.   MATTHEW 5:6, 9

Let love be your highest goal!   1 CORINTHIANS 14:1

*W*orking toward justice, peace, and love in the world
and bringing people into a relationship with God are
ambitions worthy of your time and energy.

My ambition has always been to preach the Good
News where the name of Christ has never been heard,
rather than where a church has already been started
by someone else.   ROMANS 15:20

*P*aul demonstrated a "holy ambition" to do great things
for God. A holy ambition is a vision rooted in the will
and service of God—a vision so great that only God can
accomplish it. But such ambition can turn into a selfish pursuit unless it is continually realigned with God's
Word and energized by the Holy Spirit. Unholy ambition
uses God to advance your own reputation and your own

cause. Holy ambition, however, means you offer yourself to be used by God to advance his vision and his cause.

Make it your goal to live a quiet life, minding your own business and working with your hands, just as we instructed you before. Then people who are not Christians will respect the way you live, and you will not need to depend on others.   1 THESSALONIANS 4:11-12

*A*fundamental ambition for your life should be to provide for yourself so that you will be respected by others and not be a burden to them.

DIVINE PROMISE

JOYFUL ARE PEOPLE OF INTEGRITY, WHO
FOLLOW THE INSTRUCTIONS OF THE LORD.
JOYFUL ARE THOSE WHO . . . SEARCH FOR HIM
WITH ALL THEIR HEARTS.   *Psalm 119:1-2*

Anger

MY QUESTION *for* GOD

Why do I sometimes get so angry?

A MOMENT *with* GOD

The LORD accepted Abel and his gift, but he did not accept Cain and his gift. This made Cain very angry, and he looked dejected.   GENESIS 4:4-5

"Didn't I tell you?" the king of Israel exclaimed to Jehoshaphat. "He never prophesies anything but trouble for me. . . . Put this man in prison, and feed him nothing but bread and water."   1 KINGS 22:18, 27

"Get out of the sanctuary, for you have sinned." . . . Uzziah, who was holding an incense burner, became furious.   2 CHRONICLES 26:18-19

Mordecai refused to bow down or show [Haman] respect. . . . [Haman] was filled with rage.   ESTHER 3:2, 5

You must all be quick to listen, slow to speak, and slow to get angry. Human anger does not produce the righteousness God desires. So get rid of all the filth and evil in your lives, and humbly accept the word God has planted in your hearts, for it has the power to save your souls.   JAMES 1:19-21

Anger is often a reaction to your pride being hurt. When you are confronted, rejected, ignored, or don't get your own way, anger is a defense mechanism to protect your ego. It is common to feel angry when you have been confronted about your own sinful actions because it wounds your pride. Train yourself to examine your heart whenever you become angry. Ask yourself, who is really offended in this situation? Is this about God's honor or my own pride? Allow God's Word to help you overcome your anger and grow in his will.

DIVINE PROMISE

A GENTLE ANSWER DEFLECTS ANGER, BUT HARSH WORDS MAKE TEMPERS FLARE.

Proverbs 15:1

Apathy

MY QUESTION *for* GOD

How do I fight feelings of apathy?

A MOMENT *with* GOD

God is not unjust. He will not forget how hard you have worked for him and how you have shown your love to him by caring for other believers, as you still do. Our great desire is that you will keep on loving others as long as life lasts, in order to make certain that what you hope for will come true. Then you will not become spiritually dull and indifferent.

HEBREWS 6:10-12

We must listen very carefully to the truth we have heard, or we may drift away from it.   HEBREWS 2:1

[Jesus said,] "I know all the things you do, that you are neither hot nor cold. I wish that you were one or the other! But since you are like lukewarm water, neither hot nor cold, I will spit you out of my mouth!"   REVELATION 3:15-16

$\mathcal{I}$n the book of Revelation, apathy is compared to lukewarm water. Cold water quenches thirst and refreshes a parched mouth. Hot water is used for cooking and sanitizing. But lukewarm water has little appeal. Apathy is much the same. When apathy settles in, it means that passion and purpose are gone. It is like a disease that feeds on your cares and motivations and wastes your talents and gifts. Recognizing your apathy can be a divine moment—you suddenly realize that you must change course before you become useless to God and others. Hard work, a thankful heart, and acts of service can help you fight off feelings of apathy and renew your focus on God's purpose, his call for you, and the blessings he has given you.

DIVINE PROMISE

I WILL GIVE THEM SINGLENESS OF HEART AND
PUT A NEW SPIRIT WITHIN THEM. I WILL TAKE
AWAY THEIR STONY, STUBBORN HEART AND
GIVE THEM A TENDER, RESPONSIVE HEART.
Ezekiel 11:19

Apology

MY QUESTION *for* GOD

Why is it so hard to apologize sometimes?

A MOMENT *with* GOD

The high and lofty one who lives in eternity, the Holy One, says this: "I live in the high and holy place with those whose spirits are contrite and humble. I restore the crushed spirit of the humble and revive the courage of those with repentant hearts."   ISAIAH 57:15

Confess your sins to each other and pray for each other so that you may be healed.   JAMES 5:16

Fools make fun of guilt, but the godly acknowledge it and seek reconciliation.   PROVERBS 14:9

A true apology takes genuine humility, and maintaining a humble spirit is one of the greatest struggles, especially for a leader. Apologizing requires you to realize your fault and then admit it to someone else. Leaders are supposed to "get it right," so it's tough to admit when you are wrong. It's often tempting to pretend the offense never happened or try to cover it up or avoid the person you've offended. These are signs that your heart is proud and you are unwilling to take responsibility for your actions. When was the last time you apologized to someone under your leadership? Your answer might indicate how humble your heart is. Refusing to apologize can have devastating effects in your life—soured relationships, bitterness, isolation, rage, guilt. But when you offer an apology, you can receive reconciliation, forgiveness, healing, courage, and respect. A sincere apology can only come from a humble heart. When you admit your fault and ask for forgiveness, you will experience a divine moment of God's healing working in your heart and your relationships.

DIVINE PROMISE

**PEOPLE WHO CONCEAL THEIR SINS WILL NOT
PROSPER, BUT IF THEY CONFESS AND TURN
FROM THEM, THEY WILL RECEIVE MERCY.**

Proverbs 28:13

Appearance

MY QUESTION *for* GOD

How much does appearance matter?

A MOMENT *with* GOD

Don't be concerned about the outward beauty of
fancy hairstyles, expensive jewelry, or beautiful
clothes. You should clothe yourselves instead with the
beauty that comes from within, the unfading beauty
of a gentle and quiet spirit, which is so precious
to God.   1 PETER 3:3-4

Charm is deceptive, and beauty does not last; but a
woman who fears the LORD will be greatly praised.

PROVERBS 31:30

If you listen to the word and don't obey, it is like
glancing at your face in a mirror. You see yourself,
walk away, and forget what you look like.   JAMES 1:23-24

Appearance does matter—but make sure you're
looking at the right things. Your body, face, and clothes
reflect only your outward shell, which is in a constant

in helping you overcome them. Pray for God to arm
you and equip you for battle, and you will be victorious
both in this life and in eternity.

DIVINE CHALLENGE

**HUMBLE YOURSELVES BEFORE GOD. RESIST THE
DEVIL, AND HE WILL FLEE FROM YOU.**   *James 4:7*

Assertiveness

MY QUESTION *for* GOD

Why is it appropriate for leaders to be assertive?

A MOMENT *with* GOD

"What sorrow awaits you teachers of religious law
and you Pharisees. Hypocrites! For you are careful
to tithe even the tiniest income from your herb
gardens, but you ignore the more important aspects
of the law—justice, mercy, and faith. You should
tithe, yes, but do not neglect the more important
things. Blind guides! You strain your water so you
won't accidentally swallow a gnat, but you swallow
a camel!"
                                          MATTHEW 23:23-24

*J*esus was often assertive when he spoke to the
Pharisees and other religious leaders. Assertiveness
means standing up for what is right or making known
your concerns. Leaders must be assertive. It may be

tempting to be silent or look the other way when others are making unethical choices or are speaking and
behaving in offensive, inappropriate ways. But you
must stand up for what you believe, and you should
lovingly confront others when necessary. Assertiveness
must be tempered with love and should be reserved for
upholding truth and justice, not for pursuing personal
agendas. Follow Jesus' model of assertiveness by studying his words in the Bible.

DIVINE PROMISE

THIS IS A TRUSTWORTHY SAYING, AND I
WANT YOU TO INSIST ON THESE TEACHINGS
SO THAT ALL WHO TRUST IN GOD WILL
DEVOTE THEMSELVES TO DOING GOOD. THESE
TEACHINGS ARE GOOD AND BENEFICIAL
FOR EVERYONE.   *Titus 3:8*

Authenticity

MY QUESTION *for* GOD

How can I let others see the authenticity of my faith?

A MOMENT *with* GOD

When the king of Nineveh heard what Jonah was
saying, he stepped down from his throne and took
off his royal robes. He dressed himself in burlap and
sat on a heap of ashes. Then the king and his nobles
sent this decree throughout the city: "No one, not

even the animals from your herds and flocks, may
eat or drink anything at all. People and animals alike
must wear garments of mourning, and everyone must
pray earnestly to God. They must turn from their
evil ways and stop all their violence. Who can tell?
Perhaps even yet God will change his mind and hold
back his fierce anger from destroying us."   JONAH 3:6-9

*S*ometimes we confuse repentance with a quick "I'm
sorry"—and we wonder why we still feel guilty and
don't sense the Holy Spirit's power in our lives. Sometimes we confuse good deeds with genuine compassion, and we wonder why people seem to see right
through us. Nineveh's genuine spiritual turnaround
models three dimensions of authentic faith:

1. *The emotional dimension.* The people of Nineveh
   were truly grieved by their sins. They were
   ashamed of the condition of their hearts.
2. *The relational dimension.* The Ninevites sought
   not just moral improvement but a real and
   vibrant relationship with the Lord.
3. *The behavioral dimension.* The Ninevites did more
   than mourn and pray—they turned from their
   sins and stopped doing wrong.

Authenticity means doing the right thing because you
really want to, not pretending to do it while trying to
achieve your own agenda. When you develop the three
dimensions of authentic faith, God and others will see
that your faith is genuine.

Authority

MY QUESTION *for* GOD

How can authority be abused?

A MOMENT *with* GOD

Let's build a great city for ourselves with a tower that reaches into the sky. This will make us famous.

GENESIS 11:4

O Egypt, to which of the trees of Eden will you compare your strength and glory? You, too, will be brought down to the depths with all these other nations. You will lie there among the outcasts who have died by the sword. This will be the fate of Pharaoh and all his hordes. I, the Sovereign LORD, have spoken!

EZEKIEL 31:18

It is not that we think we are qualified to do anything on our own. Our qualification comes from God.

2 CORINTHIANS 3:5

Authority can be intoxicating because it is often accompanied by recognition, control, and wealth. These things feed pride, and pride leads away from God and into sin. This is why the power that comes from authority so often corrupts. If you are in a position of authority, accountability and service will help you use it wisely. When you are held accountable for your motives and actions, you are more careful in what you say and do. When you determine to serve others rather than be served, you will gain respect and loyalty from those under your authority.

DIVINE PROMISE

WHOEVER WANTS TO BE A LEADER AMONG YOU MUST BE YOUR SERVANT.   *Matthew 20:26*

Backsliding

MY QUESTION *for* GOD

What do I do when I've fallen away from God?

A MOMENT *with* GOD

Now this is what the LORD says to the family of Israel: "Come back to me and live!"   AMOS 5:4

Everyone has sinned; we all fall short of God's glorious standard. Yet God, with undeserved kindness, declares that we are righteous. He did this through Christ Jesus when he freed us from the penalty for our sins.   ROMANS 3:23-24

Finally, I confessed all my sins to you and stopped trying to hide my guilt. I said to myself, "I will confess my rebellion to the LORD." And you forgave me! All my guilt is gone.   PSALM 32:5

Every day you have a choice to make when it comes to your relationship with God. You can step toward him or step away from him. It takes conscious effort to step toward him; it takes no effort to step away, for your sinful nature is always pulling you in the wrong direction. As a leader, it's easy to get so absorbed with keeping others on track that you neglect to keep yourself on track. Suddenly you realize you are further from God than you should be. That is a critical moment: You can either deny the problem and keep going, or you can recognize the problem and turn around. Backsliding, by definition, is slipping away from God. On the other hand, confession is reaching out to God so he can pull you in his direction. When you confess, you acknowledge that your sin has separated you from God. God forgives you and brings you back to him. Confess your inadequacies to God each day; he will forgive you and keep you close to him.

DIVINE PROMISE
IF WE CONFESS OUR SINS TO HIM, HE IS FAITHFUL AND JUST TO FORGIVE US OUR SINS AND TO CLEANSE US FROM ALL WICKEDNESS.
1 John 1:9

Balance

MY QUESTION *for* GOD

*With all my responsibilities at work and at home, how do
I achieve balance?*

A MOMENT *with* GOD

I run with purpose in every step. I am not just
shadowboxing. I discipline my body like an athlete,
training it to do what it should.   1 CORINTHIANS 9:26-27

For everything there is a season, a time for every
activity under heaven.   ECCLESIASTES 3:1

[Jesus said,] "I brought glory to you here on earth
by completing the work you gave me to do. Now,
Father, bring me into the glory we shared before the
world began."   JOHN 17:4-5

*L*iving a balanced life means honoring God, others,
and yourself through the ways you use your gifts and
spend your time and resources. Your life can get out
of balance when you focus on one of your responsibilities at the cost of others. God assures you that there
is a time for everything, including everything he calls
you to do. Look to the example of Jesus; despite his
infinite potential and all the needs around him, he left
much undone yet completed all that God had given
him to do. You will find true peace and contentment
when you realize you don't have to do everything, just
those things God created you to do. Begin each day in

prayer, asking God to show you what he wants you to get done. When you coordinate your agenda with his, your priorities will become clear, and you will find balance in your life.

DIVINE CHALLENGE
YOU ARE A SLAVE TO WHATEVER CONTROLS YOU. *2 Peter 2:19*

Betrayal

MY QUESTION *for* GOD
How should I respond when someone betrays me?

A MOMENT *with* GOD

Never take revenge. Leave that to the righteous anger of God. For the Scriptures say, "I will take revenge; I will pay them back," says the LORD. Instead, "If your enemies are hungry, feed them. If they are thirsty, give them something to drink. In doing this, you will heap burning coals of shame on their heads." Don't let evil conquer you, but conquer evil by doing good.

ROMANS 12:19-21

The worst response to betrayal is revenge. The wisest response to betrayal is to stop the cycle of retaliation by offering love instead of vengeance. Trust God to judge your cause.

Forgive us our sins, as we have forgiven those who sin against us. . . . If you forgive those who sin against you, your heavenly Father will forgive you.

MATTHEW 6:12-14

*F*orgiveness is the only healing for betrayal. No offense against you compares with your own offenses against God before he saved you. A forgiven person forgives. If you refuse to forgive others, you don't realize just how much God has forgiven you.

Look—the time has come. The Son of Man is betrayed into the hands of sinners.   MATTHEW 26:45

*R*ecognize that betrayal is an inevitable part of the human experience. Even Jesus was betrayed. This may not make betrayal any easier to accept, but it does help you gain perspective.

Get rid of all bitterness, rage, anger, harsh words, and slander, as well as all types of evil behavior. Instead, be kind to each other, tenderhearted, forgiving one another, just as God through Christ has forgiven you.   EPHESIANS 4:31-32

Esau ran to meet him and embraced him, threw his arms around his neck, and kissed him. And they both wept. . . . "My brother, I have plenty," Esau answered. "Keep what you have for yourself." But Jacob insisted, "No, if I have found favor with you, please accept this gift from me. And what a relief to see your friendly smile. It is like seeing the face of God!" GENESIS 33:4, 9-10

*J*acob betrayed his brother, Esau, but after years of separation, Esau forgave him. Peter denied knowing Jesus, but Jesus continued to love and use him (see John 18:15-18, 25-27; 21:15-19). Continue to love those who betray you. Overlook the betrayal to love and forgive the person who betrayed you. Forgiveness is powerful, and it is the only escape from the downward spiral of retaliation and revenge.

Joseph replied, "Don't be afraid of me. Am I God, that I can punish you? You intended to harm me, but God intended it all for good. He brought me to this position so I could save the lives of many people. No, don't be afraid. I will continue to take care of you and your children." So he reassured them by speaking kindly to them.   GENESIS 50:19-21

*R*ecognize God's hand in your life. Even when someone sins against you, God can pick up the pieces and make something good come out of it.

DIVINE PROMISE

[JESUS SAID,] "THOSE THE FATHER HAS GIVEN
ME WILL COME TO ME, AND I WILL NEVER
REJECT THEM." *John 6:37*

Bible

MY QUESTION *for* GOD

How can leaders use God's Word as a leadership tool?

A MOMENT *with* GOD

All Scripture is inspired by God and is useful to teach us what is true and to make us realize what is wrong in our lives. It corrects us when we are wrong and teaches us to do what is right. God uses it to prepare and equip his people to do every good work.

2 TIMOTHY 3:16-17

Scripture not only shapes leaders, but it also gives them the method for shaping the people they lead. God's Word directs the path of your spiritual journey, reveals sin, exposes the foolishness of worldly wisdom, shows you your need for God, gives you correction, shows you to the best way to live, and teaches you how to act in the power of the Spirit to remain faithful. God's Word provides the basis for your decision making, your strategy, your conduct, and your interaction with others. Leaders who intentionally teach, discipline, and disciple others with clear direction from God's Word will shape people in the most effective and productive ways.

EVEN MORE BLESSED ARE ALL WHO HEAR THE
WORD OF GOD AND PUT IT INTO PRACTICE.
Luke 11:28

Blessings

MY QUESTION *for* GOD

How can leaders bless the people they lead?

A MOMENT *with* GOD

The master was full of praise. "Well done, my
good and faithful servant. You have been faithful in
handling this small amount, so now I will give you
many more responsibilities. Let's celebrate together!"

MATTHEW 25:21

Let's not get tired of doing what is good. At just the
right time we will reap a harvest of blessing if we
don't give up.   GALATIANS 6:9

You will experience all these blessings if you obey the
LORD your God.   DEUTERONOMY 28:2

*B*lessings can be given and received. We don't talk
much today about blessing others, but it was a vital part
of life in Bible times. Blessing someone meant praising them, praying for them, and committing them to
God's care. It also meant dedicating them to God and
challenging them to be committed to him forever. God

was recognized as the ultimate source of all blessings, so if you walked with the Lord, you had his blessing. To receive God's blessing meant not only enjoying the gifts of life, joy, peace, abundance, children, home, reputation, health, freedom, work, food, and so on, but also having a deeper relationship with God. Leaders often enjoy the fruit of work well done by a group of people they lead. The leader's role is to say thank you and to bless the people in the group or organization. Giving a blessing, or receiving one, is a divine moment. Withholding praise or well-deserved remuneration cheats people and hurts them, but giving proper praise and affirmation enlarges their hearts and deepens their commitment to their leader and their work.

DIVINE PROMISE

MAY THE LORD BLESS YOU AND PROTECT YOU. MAY THE LORD SMILE ON YOU AND BE GRACIOUS TO YOU. MAY THE LORD SHOW YOU HIS FAVOR AND GIVE YOU HIS PEACE.

Numbers 6:24-26

Boundaries

MY QUESTION *for* GOD

What boundaries do I need in my life, and why do I need them?

A MOMENT *with* GOD

Guard your heart above all else, for it determines the
course of your life.   PROVERBS 4:23

My child, listen and be wise: Keep your heart on the
right course.   PROVERBS 23:19

𝒯he purpose of a guardrail on a dangerous curve is
not to inhibit your freedom to drive, but to save your
life! That guardrail keeps you on the road and provides security and safety. The Bible tells us that without
some restraints, we would go out of control. Look to
God's Word to be a guardrail as you travel through
life—not to inhibit your freedom but to keep you safe
and on the right path. If you don't guard your heart
with God's Word and stay focused on the road God has
laid out for you, you may have a terrible accident when
temptation distracts you. This also applies to business
and ministry. When you do what is right according to
God's Word, you develop a reputation of integrity. You
don't take advantage of others, you realize you can't
take credit for your successes, and you know you need
to rely on God and others to help you finish strong.
These boundaries don't restrict you but in fact help you
do well in business, in ministry, or in any area of life.

DIVINE PROMISE

JOYFUL ARE THOSE YOU DISCIPLINE, LORD,
THOSE YOU TEACH WITH YOUR INSTRUCTIONS.
Psalm 94:12

Brokenness

MY QUESTION *for* GOD

Why is brokenness a quality that a leader should develop?

A MOMENT *with* GOD

David confessed to Nathan, "I have sinned against the LORD." Nathan replied, "Yes, but the LORD has forgiven you, and you won't die for this sin."

2 SAMUEL 12:13

Have mercy on me, O God, because of your unfailing love. Because of your great compassion, blot out the stain of my sins. Wash me clean from my guilt. Purify me from my sin. For I recognize my rebellion; it haunts me day and night. Against you, and you alone, have I sinned; I have done what is evil in your sight. You will be proved right in what you say, and your judgment against me is just.   PSALM 51:1-4

The sacrifice you desire is a broken spirit. You will not reject a broken and repentant heart, O God.

PSALM 51:17

My hands have made both heaven and earth; they and everything in them are mine. I, the LORD, have spoken! I will bless those who have humble and contrite hearts, who tremble at my word.   ISAIAH 66:2

When leaders fall into sin or tough times, they must also fall to their knees. David committed adultery with

Bathsheba and then had her husband murdered—it doesn't get much worse than that. Yet when he was confronted (see 2 Samuel 12), David didn't run from God. He didn't make excuses for his failure, nor did he give up in despair. Instead, he acknowledged God's justice and cast himself on God's mercy. He even made his confession public when he wrote Psalm 51. When you experience brokenness, you become aware of your full dependence upon God. Your pride and self-sufficiency are literally broken down. Brokenness comes most often through circumstances that overwhelm you or through sin that forces you to realize that the only way out of your mess is through God's help. Those who are open about their brokenness, as David was, have a greater influence upon others who need help. If you have been broken by sin or circumstances, allow God to use your experience to help others overcome their struggles.

DIVINE PROMISE

THE LORD IS CLOSE TO THE BROKENHEARTED;
HE RESCUES THOSE WHOSE SPIRITS
ARE CRUSHED. *Psalm 34:18*

Burnout

MY QUESTION *for* GOD

I'm burning the candle at both ends. How do I find the strength to keep going when I feel I have nothing left to give?

A Moment *with* God

When David and his men were in the thick of battle, David became weak and exhausted.   2 Samuel 21:15

I am exhausted and completely crushed. My groans come from an anguished heart.   Psalm 38:8

This is what the Sovereign Lord, the Holy One of Israel, says: "Only in returning to me and resting in me will you be saved. In quietness and confidence is your strength."   Isaiah 30:15

Then Jesus said, "Come to me, all of you who are weary and carry heavy burdens, and I will give you rest. . . . You will find rest for your souls."

Matthew 11:28-29

He gives power to the weak and strength to the powerless. Even youths will become weak and tired, and young men will fall in exhaustion. But those who trust in the Lord will find new strength. They will soar high on wings like eagles. They will run and not grow weary. They will walk and not faint.

Isaiah 40:29-31

*B*urnout is overwhelming exhaustion and the inability to push on. It is often brought about by too much stress. We all experience times of burnout, when we feel tapped out emotionally, mentally, physically, and spiritually. In our fast-paced, 24-7 world, it isn't surprising that we become quickly exhausted. Because burnout can be draining and paralyzing, you need to take care of your body and mind by eating right, exercising, and getting enough sleep and relaxation. Otherwise you won't be able to function effectively. One of the best ways to reduce burnout is to take time out to be close to God. When you're overextended, you are likely neglecting your time with God. When you draw close to him, you can tap into his power, strength, peace, protection, and love. Schedule time to meditate on God's Word and read a book that challenges you spiritually. As you focus on God's priorities, you can see more clearly your own priorities and lighten your load.

DIVINE PROMISE

THE LORD IS MY SHEPHERD; I HAVE ALL THAT
I NEED. HE LETS ME REST IN GREEN MEADOWS;
HE LEADS ME BESIDE PEACEFUL STREAMS.
HE RENEWS MY STRENGTH. HE GUIDES ME
ALONG RIGHT PATHS, BRINGING HONOR
TO HIS NAME.   *Psalm 23:1-3*

Business

MY QUESTION *for* GOD

Is God interested in the success of my business?

A MOMENT *with* GOD

A Jew named Aquila . . . had recently arrived from Italy with his wife, Priscilla. . . . Paul lived and worked with them, for they were tentmakers just as he was.   ACTS 18:2-3

You know that these hands of mine have worked to supply my own needs and even the needs of those who were with me. And I have been a constant example of how you can help those in need by working hard.   ACTS 20:34-35

To enjoy your work and accept your lot in life—this is indeed a gift from God.   ECCLESIASTES 5:19

𝒫aul, Aquila, and Priscilla were Christian leaders in ministry and business. They provide us with an example of how Christians can use their business and its proceeds to serve God. God honors integrity, excellence, and hard work. While these character traits don't necessarily bring financial blessings, you can be sure that God will take special interest in any enterprise whose leaders acknowledge him and faithfully live by his standards. It is truly a divine moment when you see God acting on your behalf, even in the area of business. When you are faithful in your work and God blesses your efforts, the impact of your business will be far more significant than just a strong balance sheet.

DIVINE CHALLENGE

WORK WILLINGLY AT WHATEVER YOU DO, AS THOUGH YOU WERE WORKING FOR THE LORD RATHER THAN FOR PEOPLE. REMEMBER THAT THE LORD WILL GIVE YOU AN INHERITANCE AS YOUR REWARD, AND THAT THE MASTER YOU ARE SERVING IS CHRIST. *Colossians 3:23-24*

Call of God

MY QUESTION *for* GOD

How do I know what God is calling me to do?

A MOMENT *with* GOD

Your word is a lamp to guide my feet and a light for
my path.   PSALM 119:105

The first step in discovering your calling is getting to
know God better by reading his Word. As God communicates to you through the Bible, he will show you what
he wants you to do and where he wants you to go.

God gave these four young men an unusual aptitude
for understanding every aspect of literature and
wisdom.   DANIEL 1:17

God has given every individual special aptitudes and
abilities. Your talents and skills provide the biggest clue
as to what God wants you to do. When he calls you to
do something unique for him, he will almost always allow you to use the gifts he has given you to get the job
done. Keep honing your special abilities, and as you use
them you will see God's call for your life. Always serve
God and find ways to utilize your primary gifts.

My life is worth nothing to me unless I use it for
finishing the work assigned me by the Lord Jesus.

ACTS 20:24

*W*hen God gives you a specific calling, it fills your thoughts and gives you the passion to pursue it wholeheartedly.

Let God transform you into a new person by changing the way you think. Then you will learn to know God's will for you. ROMANS 12:2

*W*hen you let God transform you by the power of his Holy Spirit, he will literally begin to change your thoughts so that you will know what he wants you to do.

DIVINE PROMISE

GOD'S GIFTS AND HIS CALL CAN NEVER BE WITHDRAWN. *Romans 11:29*

Call of God

MY QUESTION *for* GOD

Does God call me to do specific things?

A MOMENT *with* GOD

The LORD gave me this message: "I knew you before I formed you in your mother's womb. Before you were born I set you apart and appointed you as my prophet to the nations." JEREMIAH 1:4-5

God may call you to do a certain job or to accomplish
a very specific task or ministry. When that happens,
he will make sure you know what it is. You will feel a
very strong sense that God is leading you in a certain
direction. It's up to you to respond by walking through
the door of opportunity God opens for you.

There are different kinds of spiritual gifts, but the
same Spirit is the source of them all. . . . A spiritual
gift is given to each of us so we can help each other.

1 CORINTHIANS 12:4, 7

Fully carry out the ministry God has given you.

2 TIMOTHY 4:5

God gives each of us a spiritual gift (sometimes more
than one!) and a special ministry in the church where
we can use those gifts to help and encourage others and
bring glory to his name. When you use your specific
spiritual gift (or gifts), you help fulfill the purpose for
which God made you.

Yes, each of you should remain as you were when
God called you. Are you a slave? Don't let that worry
you—but if you get a chance to be free, take it. And
remember, if you were a slave when the Lord called
you, you are now free in the Lord. And if you were
free when the Lord called you, you are now a slave
of Christ. God paid a high price for you, so don't be
enslaved by the world. Each of you, dear brothers and
sisters, should remain as you were when God first
called you.   1 CORINTHIANS 7:20-24

The call to follow Jesus does not necessarily mean a call to a specific job or Christian ministry. Sometimes your calling may simply be to obey God wherever you are right now.

Do everything you want to do; take it all in. But remember that you must give an account to God for everything you do. ECCLESIASTES 11:9

God gives you the freedom to follow many different roads and pursue many different activities over the course of your life, but remember that you will have to answer to him. Not everything you do is a call from God, but everything you do is accountable to God.

DIVINE PROMISE

NOW MAY THE GOD OF PEACE MAKE YOU HOLY IN EVERY WAY, AND MAY YOUR WHOLE SPIRIT AND SOUL AND BODY BE KEPT BLAMELESS UNTIL OUR LORD JESUS CHRIST COMES AGAIN. GOD WILL MAKE THIS HAPPEN, FOR HE WHO CALLS YOU IS FAITHFUL.   *1 Thessalonians 5:23-24*

Caution

MY QUESTION *for* GOD

How can I balance risk and caution?

A MOMENT *with* GOD

If you are afraid to attack, go down to the camp with
your servant Purah. Listen to what the Midianites are
saying, and you will be greatly encouraged. Then you
will be eager to attack.   JUDGES 7:10-11

*F*ear keeps you from taking risks. Caution keeps you
from risking too much. The first step in balancing risk
and caution is to identify what makes you afraid to take
a particular risk, then confirm whether or not that fear
is legitimate. You may be surprised at how often your
fears have no basis.

The Jews who lived near the enemy came and told us
again and again, "They will come from all directions
and attack us!" So I placed armed guards behind
the lowest parts of the wall in the exposed areas.
I stationed the people to stand guard by families,
armed with swords, spears, and bows. . . . We
carried our weapons with us at all times, even when
we went for water.   NEHEMIAH 4:12-13, 23

*A*long with examining your fears, you must be aware
of any real dangers and be prepared to face them. In this
story from the Old Testament, Nehemiah anticipated
the obstacles to the work of rebuilding the wall of Jerusalem, but he didn't let the threat of attack stop him or
the people from working! When you take caution, you
prepare for the worst, but then you work diligently.

Wise people think before they act; fools don't—and
even brag about their foolishness.   PROVERBS 13:16

The prudent understand where they are going,
but fools deceive themselves. . . . Only simpletons
believe everything they're told! The prudent carefully
consider their steps.   PROVERBS 14:8, 15

*T*oo much caution can keep you from becoming a success or fulfilling your dreams if it prevents you from
taking the first step. Don't be afraid to make a mistake.
Think about what you want to do, plan the best way to
do it, and then move ahead with confidence!

DIVINE PROMISE
THE WISE ARE CAUTIOUS AND AVOID DANGER;
FOOLS PLUNGE AHEAD WITH RECKLESS
CONFIDENCE.   *Proverbs 14:16*

Celebration

MY QUESTIONS *for* GOD
*What does God say about celebration? Is it too extravagant
for Christians?*

A MOMENT *with* GOD
Nehemiah the governor, Ezra the priest and scribe,
and the Levites who were interpreting for the people
said to them, "Don't mourn or weep on such a day as

this! For today is a sacred day before the LORD your
God." . . . Nehemiah continued, "Go and celebrate
with a feast of rich foods and sweet drinks, and share
gifts of food with people who have nothing prepared."

NEHEMIAH 8:9-10

The master said, "Well done, my good and faithful
servant. You have been faithful in handling this
small amount, so now I will give you many more
responsibilities. Let's celebrate together!"

MATTHEW 25:23

Praise him with the tambourine and dancing; praise
him with strings and flutes!   PSALM 150:4

𝓔zra and Nehemiah were godly leaders of the Israelites,
but when the people had completed the task of rebuilding the wall of Jerusalem, it was time to celebrate! God
had helped them succeed. In thanksgiving and dedica-
tion, the people listened to God's Word. This moment
of joy and gladness was also a time for food and fes-
tivities—a holy party—to remember, thank, praise,
and honor God and to dedicate themselves to him in a
celebratory spirit with feasting and sharing. When you
celebrate special days such as holidays, anniversaries,
or major milestones, include these elements, which
God's people have long used in their celebrations. You
will be blessed beyond expectation.

DIVINE PROMISE

LET ALL WHO TAKE REFUGE IN YOU REJOICE;
LET THEM SING JOYFUL PRAISES FOREVER.
SPREAD YOUR PROTECTION OVER THEM, THAT
ALL WHO LOVE YOUR NAME MAY BE FILLED
WITH JOY. *Psalm 5:11*

Challenge

MY QUESTION *for* GOD

How does God challenge me?

A MOMENT *with* GOD

Looking at the man, Jesus felt genuine love for
him. "There is still one thing you haven't done," he
told him. "Go and sell all your possessions and give
the money to the poor, and you will have treasure
in heaven. Then come, follow me." At this the
man's face fell, and he went away sad, for he had
many possessions.   MARK 10:21-22

Put me on trial, LORD, and cross-examine me. Test
my motives and my heart.   PSALM 26:2

Search me, O God, and know my heart; test me and
know my anxious thoughts.   PSALM 139:23

God challenges you to take a test—the heart test. He
wants you to examine your heart, that is, to test your
motives and discover what you value most. If God is

usually an afterthought in your life, if you give only a little time or money to your church and to God's work—you have to ask if you are passing his test. Another part of the heart test evaluates how you react to problems that come up in your life. Do you go right to God to ask for help, or do you try to solve the problems on your own without even thinking about God? Perhaps the biggest part of the heart test is asking yourself how you would respond if God asked you to give away everything to follow him. If God is challenging you in these ways, how are you handling the test?

DIVINE PROMISE

I WILL GIVE YOU A NEW HEART, AND I WILL PUT A NEW SPIRIT IN YOU. I WILL TAKE OUT YOUR STONY, STUBBORN HEART AND GIVE YOU A TENDER, RESPONSIVE HEART.   *Ezekiel 36:26*

Change

MY QUESTION *for* GOD

How do I implement change when it so often brings criticism?

A MOMENT *with* GOD

Sanballat was very angry when he learned that we were rebuilding the wall. He flew into a rage and mocked the Jews, saying in front of his friends and the Samarian army officers, "What does this bunch of poor, feeble Jews think they're doing? Do they think they can build the wall in a single day by just offering a few sacrifices? Do they actually think they can make something of stones from a rubbish heap—and charred ones at that?" Tobiah the Ammonite, who was standing beside him, remarked, "That stone wall would collapse if even a fox walked along the top of it!" Then I prayed, "Hear us, our God, for we are being mocked. May their scoffing fall back on their own heads, and may they themselves become captives in a foreign land! Do not ignore their guilt. Do not blot out their sins, for they have provoked you to anger here in front of the builders."   NEHEMIAH 4:1-5

One of the primary tasks of a leader is initiating, implementing, and responding to change. But anyone who works for change must take criticism. If no one is mad at you, you're probably not attempting to change anything of significance. Nehemiah models the way to respond when you are under fire for change. First, don't believe everything your critics say. If Nehemiah had accepted that he and his coworkers were just a "bunch of poor, feeble Jews," he would have grown disheartened. While it is important to be open to constructive criticism, it is equally important to shut out words that are meant to cut you down. Second, don't retaliate. Seeking to get even with your critics lowers you to their level and distracts you from your mission. Do as Nehemiah did: lay the injustice before the Lord, leave vengeance to him, and continue to pursue the opportunities God gives you to encourage and strengthen his people through times of change.

DIVINE PROMISE

DON'T COPY THE BEHAVIOR AND CUSTOMS OF
THIS WORLD, BUT LET GOD TRANSFORM YOU
INTO A NEW PERSON BY CHANGING THE WAY
YOU THINK. THEN YOU WILL LEARN TO KNOW
GOD'S WILL FOR YOU, WHICH IS GOOD AND
PLEASING AND PERFECT.   *Romans 12:2*

Character

MY QUESTION *for* GOD

Does a leader's character matter?

A MOMENT *with* GOD

Suppose a certain man is righteous and does what is
just and right. . . . He is a merciful creditor. . . . He
does not rob the poor but instead gives food to the
hungry and provides clothes for the needy. He . . .
stays away from injustice, is honest and fair when
judging others, and faithfully obeys my decrees and
regulations. Anyone who does these things is just and
will surely live, says the Sovereign LORD.

                                                    EZEKIEL 18:5, 7-9

Even children are known by the way they act,
whether their conduct is pure, and whether it is right.

                                                    PROVERBS 20:11

*P*eople often argue that our personal lives do not
matter as long as we perform well on the job or look

good in public. God, however, does not make a distinction between our public and private lives. Justice, righteousness, integrity, mercy, honesty, fairness, and faithfulness are the essential traits of godly character because they reflect God's character. You are a leader of good character when you display the same integrity in private as you do in public. If you demonstrate ungodly characteristics behind closed doors, you can be sure they will eventually surface for everyone to see, and your effectiveness as a leader will be seriously damaged.

DIVINE CHALLENGE

IF YOU ARE FAITHFUL IN LITTLE THINGS, YOU WILL BE FAITHFUL IN LARGE ONES. BUT IF YOU ARE DISHONEST IN LITTLE THINGS, YOU WON'T BE HONEST WITH GREATER RESPONSIBILITIES.
Luke 16:10

Commitment

MY QUESTION *for* GOD

How can I motivate others to greater commitment?

A MOMENT *with* GOD

The priests and Levites first purified themselves; then they purified the people, the gates, and the wall.

NEHEMIAH 12:30

You yourself must be an example to them by doing
good works of every kind.　　　　　　　TITUS 2:7

Take a new grip with your tired hands and strengthen
your weak knees. Mark out a straight path for your
feet so that those who are weak and lame will not fall
but become strong.　　　　　　　HEBREWS 12:12-13

𝒩o amount of criticizing or nagging can inspire
greater commitment in others. In fact, nagging produces only one guaranteed result—deafness! The
more you nag, the less people listen. The actions of
the Levites in the verse from Nehemiah are instruc-
tive. Dedicate yourself to the Lord, and then live out a
contagious commitment to God. You should also check
your motives: Are you really serving out of love for
God? Or have you become preoccupied with yourself
and irritated with people who aren't carrying their
share of the load? Divine inspiration is more likely to
come from your example than from your words.

DIVINE CHALLENGE

JESUS REPLIED, "'YOU MUST LOVE THE LORD
YOUR GOD WITH ALL YOUR HEART, ALL YOUR
SOUL, AND ALL YOUR MIND.' THIS IS THE FIRST
AND GREATEST COMMANDMENT. A SECOND IS
EQUALLY IMPORTANT: 'LOVE YOUR NEIGHBOR
AS YOURSELF.'" *Matthew 22:37-39*

Communication

MY QUESTION *for* GOD

*How does God communicate with me, and how can I
communicate with him?*

A MOMENT *with* GOD

Come close to God, and God will come close to you.

JAMES 4:8

When the Father sends the Advocate as my
representative—that is, the Holy Spirit—he
will teach you everything and will remind you of
everything I have told you.   JOHN 14:26

The heavens proclaim the glory of God. The skies
display his craftsmanship. Day after day they continue
to speak; night after night they make him known.

PSALM 19:1-2

When I discovered your words, I devoured them.
They are my joy and my heart's delight, for I bear
your name, O LORD God of Heaven's Armies.

JEREMIAH 15:16

Never stop praying.   1 THESSALONIANS 5:17

Communication with others is easier today than ever
before. We have telephones, walkie-talkies, fax ma-
chines, e-mail, GPS tracking systems, cell phones, the
Internet—even cell phones with Internet! Why? Because communication is important. We like to keep in

touch because it is vital to the quality and success of our personal and business relationships. How much more, then, should we keep in touch with God, who longs to have a close relationship with us! Do you feel you are often so busy communicating with everyone else that your communication with God becomes sporadic? How do you reestablish communication with him? Find ways to regularly communicate with him, and learn to listen as he communicates with you. Only then will you experience a breakthrough in your spiritual life.

God communicates with you through his Word, so read it daily to keep in touch with him. God communicates with you through his Son, Jesus Christ, so talk to him often during your day. God communicates with you through his Holy Spirit, so pay special attention to the way he speaks to your heart. God communicates with you through your conscience, your internal moral radar that helps you know right from wrong, so always listen to your conscience. God communicates with you through his creation, so look for God's fingerprints in his handiwork, and you won't be able to miss him. The more time you spend communicating with God, the closer and more successful your relationship with him will be.

DIVINE PROMISE

THE LORD IS CLOSE TO ALL WHO CALL ON HIM, YES, TO ALL WHO CALL ON HIM IN TRUTH. HE GRANTS THE DESIRES OF THOSE WHO FEAR HIM; HE HEARS THEIR CRIES FOR HELP AND RESCUES THEM. *Psalm 145:18-19*

Community

MY QUESTION *for* GOD

How can I help others maintain a sense of community in the midst of changes and challenges?

A MOMENT *with* GOD

My God gave me the idea to call together all the nobles and leaders of the city, along with the ordinary citizens, for registration. I had found the genealogical record of those who had first returned to Judah. This is what was written there: Here is the list of the Jewish exiles of the provinces who returned from their captivity. King Nebuchadnezzar had deported them to Babylon, but now they returned to Jerusalem and the other towns in Judah where they originally lived. Their leaders were Zerubbabel, Jeshua, Nehemiah, Seraiah, Reelaiah, Nahamani, Mordecai, Bilshan, Mispar, Bigvai, Rehum, and Baanah. This is the number of the men of Israel who returned from exile.   NEHEMIAH 7:5-7

To strengthen connectedness within a church, organization, or family, it is helpful to remember and celebrate the past. The Jews had recently returned from exile and were surrounded by hostile neighbors. They needed a strong sense of community in order to survive. Without it, their work would falter and the people would splinter. So Nehemiah published the list of the first wave of exiles who had returned under Zerubbabel in 538 BC. This gave the people a sense of continuity with the past as they faced an uncertain future.

Affirming your heritage confirms your unity. You can't live in the past, but you must build the future on it. To build a sense of community today, it is important to celebrate and remember the divine moments in the past when God did great works among his people.

DIVINE CHALLENGE

WE WILL NOT HIDE THESE TRUTHS FROM OUR CHILDREN; WE WILL TELL THE NEXT GENERATION ABOUT THE GLORIOUS DEEDS OF THE LORD, ABOUT HIS POWER AND HIS MIGHTY WONDERS.   *Psalm 78:4*

Comparisons

MY QUESTION *for* GOD

Is it okay to make comparisons?

A MOMENT *with* GOD

Oh, don't worry; we wouldn't dare say that we are as wonderful as these other men who tell you how important they are! But they are only comparing themselves with each other, using themselves as the standard of measurement. How ignorant!

2 CORINTHIANS 10:12

Now you must be holy in everything you do, just as God who chose you is holy. For the Scriptures say, "You must be holy because I am holy."   1 PETER 1:15-16

Oh, that my actions would consistently reflect your decrees! Then I will not be ashamed when I compare my life with your commands.   PSALM 119:5-6

"How do I measure up?" You have probably grappled with this question at one time or another. Satan tries to convince you to compare yourself to other people, to base your worth on how you measure up in appearance, possessions, accomplishments, or social status. But making comparisons is almost always destructive because it leads to sinful thoughts: If you think you're better than someone else, it leads to pride and selfishness. If you think you're not as good as someone else, it leads to jealousy and discouragement. Both results are unhealthy and leave you feeling either overconfident or inadequate. Worse yet, comparing yourself to others takes your focus off Jesus, whom you should be serving wholeheartedly.

A better method of determining your worth is comparing yourself to God's standards. Against his holiness, we all fall short. But nothing can compare with the grace that makes us holy in his eyes, even though we don't deserve it. In God's eyes, every person is valued and loved. Maintaining a balance between humility over sin and exultation over God's lavish grace is the best way to live and lead. God doesn't compare you with others, so neither should you. Just enjoy the grace of the God who has no comparison.

DIVINE PROMISE

PAY CAREFUL ATTENTION TO YOUR OWN
WORK, FOR THEN YOU WILL GET THE
SATISFACTION OF A JOB WELL DONE, AND
YOU WON'T NEED TO COMPARE YOURSELF TO
ANYONE ELSE. FOR WE ARE EACH RESPONSIBLE
FOR OUR OWN CONDUCT.   *Galatians 6:4-5*

Compassion

MY QUESTION *for* GOD

Should a leader have compassion?

A MOMENT *with* GOD

The LORD is compassionate and merciful, slow to get
angry and filled with unfailing love.   PSALM 103:8

Instead, be kind to each other, tenderhearted,
forgiving one another, just as God through Christ has
forgiven you.   EPHESIANS 4:32

Moved with compassion, Jesus reached out and
touched him. "I am willing," he said. "Be healed!"

                                              MARK 1:41

You must be compassionate, just as your Father
is compassionate.   LUKE 6:36

When we think of someone who has compassion, we
think of a person with a heart. A leader without compas-

sion is someone to be feared—apathetic, unmerciful, callous, heartless. Compassion is both an emotion (being moved with pity for someone) and an action (acting kindly to someone in need). Jesus felt great compassion for the crowds of people who followed him, desperately searching for meaning and healing. Jesus showed them compassion by telling them the Good News about God. Compassion is a tearing of the heart, a true caring, a quality deeply seated in your emotions that inspires you respond to another person in need. Compassion can be a litmus test of your commitment and desire to love others as Christ loves you. It is a mark of strong leadership, because those you lead have great needs. To be Christlike is to share in Christ's compassionate feelings and actions in response to the needs of others, particularly those who would suffer greater hardship without your help. If you are not moved by the needs and hurts of the people around you, you may develop a heart of stone, which could eventually become too hard to respond to others or even God. A caring and compassionate leader is a respected leader.

DIVINE PROMISE

THE FAITHFUL LOVE OF THE LORD NEVER ENDS! HIS MERCIES NEVER CEASE. GREAT IS HIS FAITHFULNESS; HIS MERCIES BEGIN AFRESH EACH MORNING. *Lamentations 3:22-23*

Competition

MY QUESTION *for* GOD

How can I use my competitive nature to serve God?

A MOMENT *with* GOD

Whatever I am now, it is all because God poured out
his special favor on me—and not without results. For
I have worked harder than any of the other apostles;
yet it was not I but God who was working through me
by his grace.   1 CORINTHIANS 15:10

Athletes cannot win the prize unless they follow
the rules.   2 TIMOTHY 2:5

Work willingly at whatever you do, as though you
were working for the Lord rather than for people.

COLOSSIANS 3:23

It's a dog-eat-dog world out there." "The winner
takes all." "Nice guys finish last." "Move up or move
over." "Winning isn't everything—it's the only thing."
These are the slogans of a world driven by competition.
When properly focused, competition can bring out the
best in you. But when infected with selfish ambition
or pride, it can destroy relationships and corrode your
heart. God's Word encourages a balanced understanding of competition. Let your competitive nature drive
you to improve yourself and sharpen your skills. The
apostle Paul is a good example of a godly person who
used his competitive nature in God's service to reach

people with the Good News about Jesus and to plant churches throughout the world. There's nothing wrong with competition. Just make sure you're not competing for the wrong goals with the wrong motives. Keep your competitive nature in check so you don't hurt someone in the process of trying to win. As a Christian, you are called to work hard to do your best, not to compete against others simply to beat them. If beating others is your only goal, you honor only yourself; you have taken your eyes off God. If doing your best is your goal, you honor the God who created you.

DIVINE CHALLENGE

DON'T YOU REALIZE THAT IN A RACE EVERYONE RUNS, BUT ONLY ONE PERSON GETS THE PRIZE? SO RUN TO WIN! ALL ATHLETES ARE DISCIPLINED IN THEIR TRAINING. THEY DO IT TO WIN A PRIZE THAT WILL FADE AWAY, BUT WE DO IT FOR AN ETERNAL PRIZE. *1 Corinthians 9:24-25*

Compromise

MY QUESTIONS *for* GOD

When is compromise appropriate? How do I reach effective compromise?

A MOMENT *with* GOD

We will follow the advice given by you and by the others who respect the commands of our God. Let it be done according to the Law of God. Get up, for it is

your duty to tell us how to proceed in setting things
straight. We are behind you.   EZRA 10:3-4

$\mathcal{I}$t is within the will of God and the wisdom of Scripture to agree to give up something for the common
good. But you must never compromise if it means acting against God's Word. It is never appropriate to compromise the will of God as revealed in Scripture.

If another believer is distressed by what you eat, you
are not acting in love if you eat it. Don't let your
eating ruin someone for whom Christ died.

ROMANS 14:15

$\mathcal{I}$n order to maintain unity in the body of Christ, a
Christian must be willing to avoid certain things. This
may require you to compromise your personal prefer-
ences, but never your Christian convictions.

Leave your sacrifice there at the altar. Go and be
reconciled to that person. Then come and offer your
sacrifice to God.   MATTHEW 5:24

$\mathcal{S}$eeking God's approval first requires reconciliation
with God's people. Reconciliation means giving up
your pride to gain peace.

We who are strong must be considerate of those who
are sensitive about things like this. We must not just
please ourselves.   ROMANS 15:1

Sometimes you must compromise so you don't offend others or cause them to stumble in their faith.

Make me truly happy by agreeing wholeheartedly with each other, loving one another, and working together with one mind and purpose.   PHILIPPIANS 2:2

Sometimes you should compromise for the sake of unity and accomplishing a common goal. This may mean giving up something you want for the sake of what the greater community wants or needs.

DIVINE PROMISE

ANYONE WHO WANDERS AWAY FROM THIS
TEACHING HAS NO RELATIONSHIP WITH
GOD. BUT ANYONE WHO REMAINS IN THE
TEACHING OF CHRIST HAS A RELATIONSHIP
WITH BOTH THE FATHER AND THE SON.
2 John 1:9

Confession

MY QUESTION *for* GOD

How can confession bring about renewal in my life?

A MOMENT *with* GOD

When I refused to confess my sin, my body wasted away, and I groaned all day long. Day and night your hand of discipline was heavy on me. My strength

evaporated like water in the summer heat. Finally,
I confessed all my sins to you and stopped trying to
hide my guilt. I said to myself, "I will confess . . . to
the LORD." And you forgave me! All my guilt is gone.

PSALM 32:3-5

*S*in often has magnified effects in the life of a leader,
perhaps because leaders feel reluctant to admit when
they are struggling with it. If you do not talk about
this struggle with God or other people, you allow sin
to fester. It distracts you, saps your energy, and causes
you to feel listless and uninspired. Leaders need renewal as much as anyone. One of the first steps toward
renewal is confession. Confession means being humble and honest with God and sincerely sorry for your
sins—both the ones you know about and the ones you
are unaware of. Confession brings God's forgiveness
and restores your relationship with him. This renews
your strength and spirit, rekindling your sense of passion for your work and compassion for those you lead.
When you confess your sin, God removes your guilt,
restores your joy, turns you in the right direction, and
heals your broken soul (and leaders often struggle with
a broken soul). A heart that truly confesses is ready for
the renewal that only God's Spirit can bring.

DIVINE PROMISE
HE RENEWS MY STRENGTH. HE GUIDES ME
ALONG RIGHT PATHS, BRINGING HONOR
TO HIS NAME. *Psalm 23:3*

Confidence

How can confidence affect my leadership?

A MOMENT *with* GOD

Elijah the prophet walked up to the altar and prayed, "O LORD, God of Abraham, Isaac, and Jacob, prove today that you are God in Israel and that I am your servant. Prove that I have done all this at your command. O LORD, answer me! Answer me so these people will know that you, O LORD, are God and that you have brought them back to yourself." Immediately the fire of the LORD flashed down from heaven and burned up the young bull, the wood, the stones, and the dust. It even licked up all the water in the trench! And when all the people saw it, they fell face down on the ground and cried out, "The LORD—he is God! Yes, the LORD is God!"

1 KINGS 18:36-39

Those who are righteous will be long remembered. They do not fear bad news; they confidently trust the LORD to care for them. They are confident and fearless and can face their foes triumphantly.

PSALM 112:6-8

Faith is the confidence that what we hope for will actually happen; it gives us assurance about things we cannot see.

HEBREWS 11:1

Confidence has many different applications. We can be confident in ourselves or our abilities, confident that something will happen, confident about certain facts (including salvation), confident in God's promises. We can also take someone into our confidence. Confidence can follow one of two courses: It can lead to pride, which results in arrogance and boasting, or it can lead to inner assurance, which produces a healthy self-esteem and a sure conviction of where you are going. The word for *confidence* is often translated in the Bible as *boldness*. With Jesus by our side, we can boldly step out in faith to do his work. We can have confidence that we can do anything within his will. Our ultimate confidence comes from trusting that God's Word is true. Then we can endure any trials we face here on earth and be sure of all the blessings that await us in heaven. A leader's confidence in God can literally change everything. Elijah's boldness on Mount Carmel began the liberation of the Israelite people from the wicked influence of idol worship. When you show your confidence that God's principles for living really work, you will have a firm foundation from which to lead, you will liberate the people you lead from unhealthy practices, ensure the positive consequences that come from godly living, and inspire others to accomplish more than they thought possible.

DIVINE PROMISE

BLESSED ARE THOSE WHO TRUST IN THE LORD AND HAVE MADE THE LORD THEIR HOPE AND CONFIDENCE. *Jeremiah 17:7*

Conflict

MY QUESTION *for* GOD

What are some biblical ways to resolve conflict?

A MOMENT *with* GOD

Abram said to Lot, "Let's not allow this conflict to
come between us or our herdsmen. After all, we are
close relatives! The whole countryside is open to you.
Take your choice of any section of the land you want,
and we will separate."   GENESIS 13:8-9

*R*esolving conflict takes initiative; someone must
make the first move. Abram gave Lot first pick of the
land, putting peace above personal desires.

Isaac's men then dug another well, but again there
was a dispute over it. . . . Isaac moved on and dug
another well. This time there was no dispute over it.

GENESIS 26:21-22

*R*esolving conflict takes humility, persistence, and a
preference for peace over personal victory.

That was the beginning of a long war between those
who were loyal to Saul and those loyal to David.

2 SAMUEL 3:1

*R*esolving conflict involves compromise. The two
sides must find common ground that is greater than

their differences. If neither side is willing to take the initiative or show the necessary humility to accomplish this, conflict can result in broken friendships, broken marriages, even all-out war.

To have such lawsuits with one another is a defeat for you. Why not just accept the injustice and leave it at that? Why not let yourselves be cheated?

1 CORINTHIANS 6:7

*Y*ou might have to give up your rights in order to resolve a conflict of interest, especially when it involves other Christians.

I pray that they will all be one, just as you and I are one—as you are in me, Father, and I am in you.

JOHN 17:21

*P*raying for peace and unity with others helps resolve conflict because you are seeking the help of the great Peacemaker.

Barnabas . . . wanted to take along John Mark. But Paul disagreed strongly. . . . Their disagreement was so sharp that they separated.   ACTS 15:37-39

*C*onflict begins when people with two opposing viewpoints are not willing to find common ground. Sometimes differences of opinion are so strong that no resolution is possible, and a parting of ways is necessary. But even in these cases, you can pray that God will bring good out of the painful experience.

A servant of the Lord must not quarrel but must be kind to everyone, be able to teach, and be patient with difficult people. Gently instruct those who oppose the truth. 2 TIMOTHY 2:24-25

*W*hen someone disagrees with you, maintain a gracious, gentle, and patient attitude instead of becoming angry or defensive.

You have heard the law that says, "Love your neighbor" and hate your enemy. But I say, love your enemies! Pray for those who persecute you! In that way, you will be acting as true children of your Father in heaven. MATTHEW 5:43-45

*H*uman nature wants to love friends and hate enemies. But Jesus taught a new perspective—the only way to resolve some conflicts is to reach out in love to your enemy. This kind of love will actually turn some enemies into friends.

If another believer sins against you, go privately and point out the offense. If the other person listens and confesses it, you have won that person back. But if you are unsuccessful, take one or two others with you and go back again, so that everything you say may be confirmed by two or three witnesses. If the person still refuses to listen, take your case to the church.

MATTHEW 18:15-17

*J*esus outlines a three-step process for confronting and resolving major conflicts between believers. This biblical solution begins with private confrontation.

DIVINE PROMISE

HE RANSOMS ME AND KEEPS ME SAFE FROM THE BATTLE WAGED AGAINST ME, THOUGH MANY STILL OPPOSE ME. *Psalm 55:18*

Confrontation

MY QUESTION *for* GOD

Why is it important to confront others when they've done something wrong?

A MOMENT *with* GOD

The next morning David wrote a letter to Joab and gave it to Uriah to deliver. The letter instructed Joab, "Station Uriah on the front lines where the battle is fiercest. Then pull back so that he will be killed." . . . So the LORD sent Nathan the prophet to tell David this story. . . . David was furious. "As surely as the LORD lives," he vowed, "any man who would do such a thing deserves to die! He must repay four lambs to the poor man for the one he stole and for having no pity." Then Nathan said to David, "You are that man! . . . Why, then, have you despised the word of the LORD and done this horrible deed? For you have murdered Uriah the Hittite with the sword of the Ammonites and stolen his wife. . . . Then David confessed to Nathan, "I have sinned against the LORD." Nathan replied, "Yes, but the LORD has forgiven you, and you won't die for this sin."   2 SAMUEL 11:14-15; 12:1, 5-9, 13

If another believer sins, rebuke that person; then if there is repentance, forgive.   LUKE 17:3

If another believer sins against you, go privately and point out the offense. If the other person listens and confesses it, you have won that person back. But if you are unsuccessful, take one or two others with you and go back again, so that everything you say may be confirmed by two or three witnesses.   MATTHEW 18:15-16

God has not given us a spirit of fear and timidity, but of power, love, and self-discipline.   2 TIMOTHY 1:7

We usually think of confrontation as negative and something to avoid. Being confronted or confronting someone else is awkward and tense. These awkward feelings make it seem that confrontation is a bad thing, but the Bible tells us differently. Confrontation can in fact be good and helpful. Nathan confronted David with his secret sins of adultery and murder. Jesus himself was confrontational when important issues were at stake. He confronted the Pharisees about their arrogance and his disciples about their lack of faith. The role of confrontation is not to criticize but to teach and correct. When confrontation is approached with a desire to help rather than hurt, it becomes a valuable tool to bring about much-needed resolution to a problem or to bring someone back to Christ and Christian living. Everyone gets off track once in a while. Confrontation can be a divine moment when the person being confronted humbly acknowledges the gap between what they're doing and what they should be doing—and then takes corrective action. Without confrontation, rarely is it possible for difficult situations to be transformed into positive results.

DIVINE CHALLENGE
PATIENTLY CORRECT, REBUKE, AND ENCOURAGE YOUR PEOPLE WITH GOOD TEACHING.
2 Timothy 4:2

Conscience

MY QUESTION *for* GOD

How does my conscience help me?

A MOMENT *with* GOD

Speaking among themselves, they said, "Clearly we are being punished because of what we did to Joseph long ago. We saw his anguish when he pleaded for his life, but we wouldn't listen."   GENESIS 42:21

Cling to your faith in Christ, and keep your conscience clear. For some people have deliberately violated their consciences; as a result, their faith has been shipwrecked.   1 TIMOTHY 1:19

My conscience is clear, but that doesn't prove I'm right. It is the Lord himself who will examine me and decide.   1 CORINTHIANS 4:4

*Y*our conscience helps you understand when you have fallen out of line with God's will. It is God's gift to each of us to keep us sensitive to his moral code. But you must use the gift. If you don't listen to and obey your conscience, it will become harder and harder to hear it. It can even malfunction if not properly cared for. It can become a flawed witness that may condemn you too harshly or let you off too easily. Your conscience will only function effectively when you stay close to God, spend time in his Word, and make an effort to understand your own tendencies toward right and wrong. If your conscience is working faithfully, it will direct your heart and mind to determine right from wrong. It will give you a strong inner sense, a voice of accountability, toward what is right. If you do not have a reputation for doing the right thing or if you are unmoved by evil or injustice, it may indicate that your conscience has become weak or inactive. Leaders without a conscience will harm those they lead. Let God sharpen and resensitize your conscience through his holy Word. Then your conscience will speak to you in harmony with God himself.

DIVINE CHALLENGE

I ALWAYS TRY TO MAINTAIN A CLEAR CONSCIENCE BEFORE GOD AND ALL PEOPLE.
Acts 24:16

Consequences

MY QUESTION for GOD

What is the value of thinking through the consequences of my words and actions?

A MOMENT with GOD

To the man [God] said, "Since you . . . ate from the tree whose fruit I commanded you not to eat, the ground is cursed because of you. All your life you will struggle to scratch a living from it."   GENESIS 3:17

The tongue can bring death or life; those who love to talk will reap the consequences.   PROVERBS 18:21

Those who live only to satisfy their own sinful nature will harvest decay and death from that sinful nature. But those who live to please the Spirit will harvest everlasting life from the Spirit.   GALATIANS 6:8

"These are the choices the LORD has given you. . . . Decide what answer I should give the LORD who sent me." "I'm in a desperate situation!" David replied.

1 CHRONICLES 21:11-13

You will always harvest what you plant.   GALATIANS 6:7

A gun fires, a bullet flies, and a person in its path dies. That death is the consequence of someone pulling the trigger of a loaded weapon. Similarly, hurtful words may be spoken that inflict wounds upon someone else. On the other hand, helpful words may be spoken that lead a person to Christ. In both cases, the words produce consequences. A consequence is an outcome, aftermath, or result. Some words or actions result in consequences that are neither morally good nor bad. For example, when you take a shower, the consequence is that you get clean. But many words and actions have definite good or bad consequences. Sin always causes bad consequences. Faithfulness to God always results in good consequences, even if they can't be seen immediately. Before you act, ask yourself, what will be the consequences of these words or actions?

DIVINE CHALLENGE

PLANT THE GOOD SEEDS OF RIGHTEOUSNESS, AND YOU WILL HARVEST A CROP OF LOVE. PLOW UP THE HARD GROUND OF YOUR HEARTS, FOR NOW IS THE TIME TO SEEK THE LORD, THAT HE MAY COME AND SHOWER RIGHTEOUSNESS UPON YOU. *Hosea 10:12*

Control

MY QUESTION *for* GOD

Is it possible to exercise control without being controlling?

A MOMENT *with* GOD

Now listen! Today I am giving you a choice between life and death, between prosperity and disaster. For I command you this day to love the LORD your God

and to keep his commands. . . . If you do this, you
will live and multiply, and the LORD your God will
bless you and the land you are about to enter and
occupy. But if your heart turns away and you refuse
to listen, and if you are drawn away to serve and
worship other gods, then I warn you now that you
will certainly be destroyed.   DEUTERONOMY 30:15-18

Commit your actions to the LORD, and your plans
will succeed.   PROVERBS 16:3

When it was clear that we couldn't persuade him, we
gave up and said, "The Lord's will be done." ACTS 21:14

*L*eaders are responsible for people without taking responsibility from them. In other words, leaders should
lead and guide, but the people they are leading should
do for themselves those things they are responsible for.
This is being in control without being controlling. Moses
did all he could to persuade the Israelites to choose to
live by God's commands, but in the end he knew that
the choice was theirs to make. If you are a leader in any
capacity—parent, teacher, supervisor, church elder,
board member—you have the responsibility to lead by
doing and saying everything you can to persuade others
to move in the right direction. After you have done your
best to guide others, you must let go and trust God to
complete the work he asked you to start.

DIVINE PROMISE

THOSE WHO ARE DOMINATED BY THE SINFUL
NATURE THINK ABOUT SINFUL THINGS, BUT
THOSE WHO ARE CONTROLLED BY THE HOLY
SPIRIT THINK ABOUT THINGS THAT PLEASE
THE SPIRIT.   *Romans 8:5*

Convictions

MY QUESTION *for* GOD

How can strong convictions help me as a leader?

A MOMENT *with* GOD

In those days Israel had no king; all the people did
whatever seemed right in their own eyes.   JUDGES 21:25

At the sound of the musical instruments, all the
people, whatever their race or nation or language,
bowed to the ground and worshiped the gold statue
that King Nebuchadnezzar had set up.   DANIEL 3:7

He guards the paths of the just and protects those
who are faithful to him. Then you will understand
what is right, just, and fair, and you will find the right
way to go.   PROVERBS 2:8-9

Let the Holy Spirit guide your lives. Then you won't
be doing what your sinful nature craves. The sinful
nature wants to do evil, which is just the opposite of
what the Spirit wants. And the Spirit gives us desires
that are the opposite of what the sinful nature desires.

GALATIANS 5:16-17

*W*ithout godly personal convictions, you would have no guidelines for living. With no guidelines for living, it would be impossible to honor God and lead others in God-pleasing ways. With no guidelines, people end up doing what seems right in their own eyes rather than doing what God commands and desires. This leads to decisions and actions based on pride and personal gratification, which ends in disaster. Every day you are faced with opportunities to choose right or wrong, good or bad, God's way or the way of the world. Practice choosing God's way, and you will develop stronger convictions. Be tenacious, and Satan cannot take over any territory in your heart. Be committed to winning any battles over your convictions. Each victory is a divine moment.

DIVINE CHALLENGE

BE ON GUARD. STAND FIRM IN THE FAITH.
BE COURAGEOUS. BE STRONG.   *1 Corinthians 16:13*

Courage

MY QUESTION *for* GOD

Why should leaders have courage?

A MOMENT *with* GOD

Then the LORD commissioned Joshua son of Nun with these words: "Be strong and courageous, for you must bring the people of Israel into the land I swore to give them. I will be with you."   DEUTERONOMY 31:23

Jesus spoke to them at once. "Don't be afraid," he said. "Take courage! I am here!"   MARK 6:50

Our God gave us the courage to declare his Good News to you boldly, in spite of great opposition.

1 THESSALONIANS 2:2

We are God's house, if we keep our courage and remain confident in our hope in Christ.   HEBREWS 3:6

*C*ourage is the ability to act on what you know is right and good, to dare to do what must be done, often in the face of danger and threats. Fear paralyzes, but courage mobilizes. Courage does not conquer fear; it simply renders fear ineffective. It gives you the confident assurance that you can succeed. Christian leaders recognize the importance of motivating people to move forward with courage to accomplish good for God and his kingdom. If you gain ground, Satan and his forces lose ground. When you recognize that you have the extra resource of God's promised help in time of need, you should have the courage to face any situation that comes your way. Sometimes the courageous thing to do is run, if it means avoiding sin or bringing about the greatest good (see Genesis 39:6-12). The Bible speaks of having courage to stand firm against evil, to remain strong in the faith, to resist temptation, and to do the right thing. When you have the courage to teach others to rely on God, the more courageous they will become, and the more everyone will see God acting on behalf of his people.

DIVINE PROMISE

BE STRONG AND COURAGEOUS! DO NOT
BE AFRAID OR DISCOURAGED. FOR THE
LORD YOUR GOD IS WITH YOU WHEREVER
YOU GO.   *Joshua 1:9*

Crisis

MY QUESTION *for* GOD

How should leaders respond to crisis?

A MOMENT *with* GOD

We worked early and late, from sunrise to sunset.
And half the men were always on guard. I also told
everyone living outside the walls to stay in Jerusalem.
That way they and their servants could help with
guard duty at night and work during the day. During
this time, none of us—not I, nor my relatives, nor
my servants, nor the guards who were with me—
ever took off our clothes. We carried our weapons
with us at all times, even when we went for water.

NEHEMIAH 4:21-23

*A*s he led his people in the face of a potential attack,
Nehemiah modeled two qualities of a good leader: perseverance and preparation. Nehemiah persevered because he never lost sight of his vision or stopped moving
toward its accomplishment. He prepared by anticipat-
ing the various forms of attack and equipping his people

to defend themselves. They were on guard, armed, and
ready. They were mobilized to work together through
the crisis. In the face of crisis, good leaders are able
to unify their people to persevere in their work while
preparing in advance for potential problems.

DIVINE PROMISE

I AM CERTAIN THAT GOD, WHO BEGAN THE
GOOD WORK WITHIN YOU, WILL CONTINUE
HIS WORK UNTIL IT IS FINALLY FINISHED ON
THE DAY WHEN CHRIST JESUS RETURNS.

Philippians 1:6

Criticism

MY QUESTION *for* GOD

Is criticism helpful or harmful?

A MOMENT *with* GOD

Why do you condemn another believer? Why do you
look down on another believer? Remember, we will
all stand before the judgment seat of God. ROMANS 14:10

Don't speak evil against each other, dear brothers
and sisters. If you criticize and judge each other, then
you are criticizing and judging God's law. But your
job is to obey the law, not to judge whether it applies
to you.   JAMES 4:11

Some people make cutting remarks, but the words of
the wise bring healing.   PROVERBS 12:18

A gentle answer deflects anger, but harsh words make
tempers flare.   PROVERBS 15:1

*W*hen you offer constructive criticism, it can be a
welcome and wholesome gift—a divine moment—if
it is given in the spirit of love. But if your criticism
ridicules, demeans, or judges, it has harmful consequences: It tears down the person's self-esteem, making him or her feel shamed and worthless; it damages
your reputation, making you look mean and merciless;
it damages your ability to offer helpful advice because
others will tend to become defensive; and it brings
greater judgment upon yourself from God, who detests
it when you hurt others. Before criticizing someone,
take an inventory of your own sins and shortcomings
so that you can approach the person with humility and
understanding.

DIVINE CHALLENGE

FIRST GET RID OF THE LOG IN YOUR OWN EYE;
THEN YOU WILL SEE WELL ENOUGH TO DEAL
WITH THE SPECK IN YOUR FRIEND'S EYE.

Matthew 7:5

Decisions

MY QUESTION for GOD

What principles should I keep in mind when making decisions?

A MOMENT with GOD

Fear of the LORD is the foundation of true knowledge, but fools despise wisdom and discipline.

PROVERBS 1:7

Good leaders make decisions with humility and reverence for God.

Rehoboam rejected the advice of the older men and instead asked the opinion of the young men who had grown up with him and were now his advisers.

1 KINGS 12:8

Fools think their own way is right, but the wise listen to others.

PROVERBS 12:15

Leaders have many people offering them advice. If you consistently reject the advice of wise counselors, like Rehoboam did, you might make foolish decisions. But if you listen to the advice of others and weigh it against God's Word, you are more likely to make good choices. Leaders should remember that being open to good advice is not a sign of weakness or inadequacy but rather shows wisdom.

What do you benefit if you gain the whole world but lose your own soul? Is anything worth more than your soul?   MATTHEW 16:26

*L*eaders must resist the temptation to make decisions out of a desire for personal gain. Such ambition eventually leads to bad decisions and unethical behavior.

One day soon afterward Jesus went up on a mountain to pray, and he prayed to God all night. At daybreak he called together all of his disciples and chose twelve of them to be apostles.   LUKE 6:12-13

*L*eaders need to saturate their decisions with prayer. This is especially true for decisions concerning the selection and care of those with whom you will work closely.

The Holy Spirit produces this kind of fruit in our lives: love, joy, peace, patience, kindness, goodness, faithfulness, gentleness, and self-control. There is no law against these things!   GALATIANS 5:22-23

*G*ood decisions are always in keeping with the traits that the Holy Spirit cultivates in you, while bad decisions often mean you are rejecting his influence on your heart.

Show me the right path, O LORD; point out the road for me to follow.   PSALM 25:4

Your laws please me; they give me wise advice.

PSALM 119:24

*K*nowing Scripture and gleaning wisdom from it give you clear direction in your decision making and provide you with the discernment you need to make the best choices. A good decision is one that is consistent with the principles found in God's Word.

DIVINE PROMISE

IF YOU NEED WISDOM, ASK OUR GENEROUS GOD, AND HE WILL GIVE IT TO YOU. HE WILL NOT REBUKE YOU FOR ASKING. BUT WHEN YOU ASK HIM, BE SURE THAT YOUR FAITH IS IN GOD ALONE. DO NOT WAVER, FOR A PERSON WITH DIVIDED LOYALTY IS AS UNSETTLED AS A WAVE OF THE SEA THAT IS BLOWN AND TOSSED BY THE WIND. *James 1:5-6*

Defeat

MY QUESTIONS *for* GOD

How am I vulnerable to defeat? Can I protect myself from being defeated?

A MOMENT *with* GOD

Israel violated the instructions about the things set apart for the LORD. A man named Achan had stolen some of these dedicated things, so the LORD was very angry with the Israelites. . . . Then Joshua said to

Achan, "My son, give glory to the LORD, the God of Israel, by telling the truth. Make your confession and tell me what you have done. Don't hide it from me." Achan replied, "It is true! I have sinned against the LORD, the God of Israel. Among the plunder I saw a beautiful robe from Babylon, 200 silver coins, and a bar of gold weighing more than a pound. I wanted them so much that I took them. They are hidden in the ground beneath my tent, with the silver buried deeper than the rest.". . . Then Joshua said to Achan, "Why have you brought trouble on us? The LORD will now bring trouble on you."   JOSHUA 7:1, 19-21, 25

*A*chan had been faithful enough to get to the Promised Land. What went wrong? He became greedy. While the Israelites were enjoying their victory in the battle of Jericho, Achan was suffering defeat in the battle for his heart. You must constantly be on guard against the attacks Satan launches at your very soul. Life's biggest conflicts don't happen in the boardroom but in the heart. When you daily evaluate the condition of your heart, you will fortify yourself against sin and temptation. Even when you are winning the physical, earthly battles in your life, don't allow temptation to defeat you in the spiritual battle for your soul.

DIVINE PROMISE

THE LORD IS FAITHFUL; HE WILL STRENGTHEN YOU AND GUARD YOU FROM THE EVIL ONE.

2 Thessalonians 3:3

Delegation

MY QUESTION *for* GOD

*What are the benefits of delegating and sharing
responsibility?*

A MOMENT *with* GOD

Moses replied, ". . . The people come to me to get a
ruling from God. When a dispute arises, they come
to me, and I am the one who settles the case between
the quarreling parties. I inform the people of God's
decrees and give them his instructions." "This is
not good!" Moses' father-in-law exclaimed. "You're
going to wear yourself out—and the people, too.
This job is too heavy a burden for you to handle all
by yourself."   EXODUS 18:15-18

[Jesus] called his twelve disciples together and began
sending them out two by two.   MARK 6:7

Moses was an enormously gifted leader, but he fell
into the trap of believing he had to do it all himself.
It is possible to be *too* responsible. When you stretch
yourself too thin, you put yourself and others at risk.
You can wear yourself out, make others wait, prevent
people from having the opportunity to use their gifts,
and keep them from growing spiritually by serving
others. In the process, people become dissatisfied and
distracted, and God's work is delayed. Jethro's advice to Moses in the book of Exodus offers us a godly
strategy for leading people and getting things done:

delegate and disciple. Delegation can provide a divine
moment for those who are assigned the task because
it stretches them, causes them to rely on God, helps
them feel useful, and inspires them to catch the vision
of their leaders.

DIVINE CHALLENGE

JESUS CAME AND TOLD HIS DISCIPLES, "I HAVE
BEEN GIVEN ALL AUTHORITY IN HEAVEN
AND ON EARTH. THEREFORE, GO AND MAKE
DISCIPLES OF ALL THE NATIONS, BAPTIZING
THEM IN THE NAME OF THE FATHER AND THE
SON AND THE HOLY SPIRIT. TEACH THESE NEW
DISCIPLES TO OBEY ALL THE COMMANDS I
HAVE GIVEN YOU."   *Matthew 28:18-20*

Dependence

MY QUESTION *for* GOD

How can I learn to depend more on God?

A MOMENT *with* GOD

My God gave me the idea to call together all the
nobles and leaders of the city, along with the ordinary
citizens, for registration.   NEHEMIAH 7:5

Nehemiah gave God credit for the idea to register the
people. This is different from the glib way that some

people say, "The Lord told me . . ." to support their own plans or opinions. Rather, Nehemiah lived with a constant sense of God's presence. His life was a moment-by-moment conversation with God, even as he energetically pursued his ambitious agenda. There are many simple strategies you can use to grow more aware of God's involvement in your life and depend on him more. Try placing a note on your telephone reminding you to say a quick prayer whenever you pick up the receiver. Or set the alarm on your watch to sound every sixty minutes; when it goes off, take thirty seconds to review how the Lord has been with you the last hour, and ask him to help you in the hour ahead. Growing more dependent upon God will only be hindered by your own inattention, not God's.

DIVINE PROMISE

BLESSED ARE THOSE WHO TRUST IN THE LORD AND HAVE MADE THE LORD THEIR HOPE AND CONFIDENCE. THEY ARE LIKE TREES PLANTED ALONG A RIVERBANK, WITH ROOTS THAT REACH DEEP INTO THE WATER. SUCH TREES ARE NOT BOTHERED BY THE HEAT OR WORRIED BY LONG MONTHS OF DROUGHT. THEIR LEAVES STAY GREEN, AND THEY NEVER STOP PRODUCING FRUIT. *Jeremiah 17:7-8*

Depression

*When I feel depressed, what can I do to reverse the downward
spiral of emotions?*

A MOMENT *with* GOD

Great is the LORD! He is most worthy of praise! He is
to be feared above all gods.   1 CHRONICLES 16:25

He comforts us in all our troubles so that we can
comfort others. When they are troubled, we will be
able to give them the same comfort God has given us.

2 CORINTHIANS 1:4

Depression often involves a kind of self-obsession in
which all you are able to see is your own problems,
pain, and despair. When you withdraw into yourself
this way, it becomes nearly impossible to see things
clearly. In fact, it becomes nearly impossible to do anything. You can't see outward, to the people you lead;
you only look inward, to your pain and hurt. One way
to deal with depression and stop the negative cycle is
to start praising God for everything you can think of:
his greatness, his love, all he has done for you, how
valuable you are to him. It may even be helpful for you
to offer comfort to others in need. Praising God will
draw your focus away from yourself, and helping others
will put your problems in perspective.

DIVINE PROMISE

MAY YOUR GRACIOUS SPIRIT LEAD ME
FORWARD ON A FIRM FOOTING.   *Psalm 143:10*

Differences

MY QUESTION *for* GOD

How can I use people's differences to strengthen my team?

A MOMENT *with* GOD

As iron sharpens iron, so a friend sharpens a friend.

PROVERBS 27:17

So it is with Christ's body. We are many parts of one
body, and we all belong to each other.   ROMANS 12:5

Why did God make people so different? Because it
is through each person's uniqueness that we can work
together to accomplish important and significant tasks.
The Bible tells us that God made each of us with a
unique set of abilities and gifts so that we can benefit the church and culture and advance his kingdom.
When we use our unique abilities, we feel significant
and worthwhile. God wants us to learn how to use our
differences to work effectively with others. Teamwork
is most effective when everyone's differences comple-
ment each other and make the team better. The team
will function like a well-oiled machine when everyone
understands how their unique contribution is essential

to the whole. The church should be the ultimate example of people with many differences coming together to work in harmony and accomplish great things. When a group of people come together to solve a problem, their differences are necessary to ensure that all angles are thought through, new ideas introduced, rough ideas sharpened, and a final solution agreed upon. The result is far better than what one individual could have done. Too often we let our differences cause confusion, conflict, and tension. We feel misunderstood. We feel like our ideas or contributions should be more important. One of your greatest challenges as a leader is to remember why God made people different and then focus on how their differences can work together. Don't allow differences to set your team members against each other. Strive to use their differences to bring them together to accomplish more than you ever thought possible.

DIVINE PROMISE

HOW WONDERFUL AND PLEASANT IT IS WHEN BROTHERS LIVE TOGETHER IN HARMONY! FOR HARMONY IS AS PRECIOUS AS THE ANOINTING OIL. . . . HARMONY IS AS REFRESHING AS THE DEW. . . . AND THERE THE LORD HAS PRONOUNCED HIS BLESSING, EVEN LIFE EVERLASTING *Psalm 133:1-3*

Disagreements

My Question *for* God

How should I handle disagreements?

A Moment *with* God

After some time Paul said to Barnabas, "Let's go back and visit each city where we previously preached the word of the Lord, to see how the new believers are doing." Barnabas agreed and wanted to take along John Mark. But Paul disagreed strongly. . . . Their disagreement was so sharp that they separated. Barnabas took John Mark with him and sailed for Cyprus. Paul chose Silas, and as he left, the believers entrusted him to the Lord's gracious care. Acts 15:36-40

God blesses those who work for peace, for they will be called the children of God.   Matthew 5:9

Jesus clearly stated that we should make every effort to resolve conflicts with one another. When disagreements arise, try to understand how the other person came to his or her position, and determine what views or goals you have in common. If you each have the same goal, see if you can both compromise some things in order to accomplish it. Sometimes you may have to agree to disagree. Do so with respect and love, agreeing to honor God even in your disagreement. God will then use your efforts for good. Paul and Barnabas had such a sharp disagreement that they decided to separate, but God used this separation to double their efforts by creating two strong missionary teams. God can still work out his will through disagreements, even when you can't see a solution.

DIVINE CHALLENGE

DON'T GET INVOLVED IN FOOLISH, IGNORANT
ARGUMENTS THAT ONLY START FIGHTS.
A SERVANT OF THE LORD MUST NOT QUARREL
BUT MUST BE KIND TO EVERYONE.   *2 Timothy 2:23-24*

Discernment

MY QUESTION *for* GOD

How can I learn discernment?

A MOMENT *with* GOD

I want you to understand what really matters, so that you may live pure and blameless lives until the day of Christ's return.   PHILIPPIANS 1:10

You need someone to teach you again the basic things about God's word. You are like babies who need milk and cannot eat solid food. For someone who lives on milk is still an infant and doesn't know how to do what is right. Solid food is for those who are mature, who through training have the skill to recognize the difference between right and wrong.   HEBREWS 5:12-14

Give me understanding and I will obey your
instructions; I will put them into practice with all
my heart.   PSALM 119:34

*D*iscernment involves disciplining your conscience,
mind, senses, and body to distinguish between right
and wrong. The Bible tells us that discernment is necessary for spiritual maturity, and that recognizing the
difference between right and wrong is a developed
skill. When you grow and mature in your faith, you
learn to recognize temptation before it overwhelms
you. You also learn to recognize truth from falsehood
and distinguish God's voice from other voices. Knowing Scripture helps you discern when someone is using
a Bible verse incorrectly. When you practice discernment and train yourself to detect right from wrong,
you can avoid the pitfalls that so many leaders fall into.
Your living and leading are better because you are following God's ways.

DIVINE PROMISE

TUNE YOUR EARS TO WISDOM, AND
CONCENTRATE ON UNDERSTANDING. CRY OUT
FOR INSIGHT, AND ASK FOR UNDERSTANDING.
SEARCH FOR THEM AS YOU WOULD FOR
SILVER; SEEK THEM LIKE HIDDEN TREASURES.
THEN YOU WILL UNDERSTAND WHAT IT
MEANS TO FEAR THE LORD, AND YOU WILL
GAIN KNOWLEDGE OF GOD. FOR THE LORD
GRANTS WISDOM! FROM HIS MOUTH COME
KNOWLEDGE AND UNDERSTANDING. *Proverbs 2:2-6*

Discipline

MY QUESTION *for* GOD

How should I discipline those I lead?

A MOMENT *with* GOD

Those who spare the rod of discipline hate their
children. Those who love their children care enough
to discipline them.   PROVERBS 13:24

*D*iscipline with love. Discipline is about relationships,
not rules. It's about safety, not retaliation. Your goal is
restoration, not revenge; teaching, not taunting.

Discipline your children while there is hope.
Otherwise you will ruin their lives.   PROVERBS 19:18

*D*iscipline right away—before it is too late. Timely discipline puts people back on track. When they wander off
the path, it's much easier to find it again if they've gone
just a few feet away from it. But if they've gone far off the
path, it's more difficult to find it again. Then they are in
danger of getting so far off track that you won't be able
to lead them back.

Fathers, do not provoke your children to anger by the
way you treat them. Rather, bring them up with the
discipline and instruction that comes from the Lord.

                                          EPHESIANS 6:4

Never discipline in anger. It is difficult to make good decisions when you are consumed by anger and your emotions drive your thinking. Discipline given in anger is often spiteful and harsh and brings shame rather than restoration.

Fathers, do not aggravate your children, or they will become discouraged.   COLOSSIANS 3:21

Discipline without causing aggravation and discouragement. Disciplinary measures may cause conflict because the person who is disciplined will probably become angry. But aggravation is different. It is caused by constant nagging that implies a person will never be good enough or will never get it right. It attacks a person's sense of value and worth instead of focusing on the behavior that needs to be corrected.

Our earthly fathers disciplined us for a few years, doing the best they knew how. But God's discipline is always good for us, so that we might share in his holiness.   HEBREWS 12:10

Discipline with godly wisdom. Every leader makes some mistakes when disciplining the people they lead. Since God's discipline is always best, you need to constantly seek his wisdom. God's wisdom comes from his Word, but it also comes from other godly people who immerse themselves in his Word and who practice appropriate discipline.

Discipline

MY QUESTION *for* GOD

How should I handle discipline among Christians?

A MOMENT *with* GOD

If another believer sins against you, go privately and point out the offense. If the other person listens and confesses it, you have won that person back. But if you are unsuccessful, take one or two others with you and go back again, so that everything you say may be confirmed by two or three witnesses. If the person still refuses to listen, take your case to the church. Then if he or she won't accept the church's decision, treat that person as a pagan or a corrupt tax collector.

MATTHEW 18:15-17

Most of you opposed him, and that was punishment enough. Now, however, it is time to forgive and comfort him.   2 CORINTHIANS 2:6-7

When we think of discipline, we often think of punishment. But that is only a small part of the biblical concept of discipline. Discipline in the Bible is goal oriented: It is meant to help and motivate someone to walk in a closer relationship with God. We tend to think of discipline in a negative way—it keeps people in line and stops bad behavior. But the true heart of discipline is positive—it disciples people, helping people become followers, particularly followers of Christ. The emphasis should be on loving guidance and teaching.

If another believer has sinned against you or fallen into a sinful habit, then go to that person and confront him or her in private. If the person won't listen, and you are convinced there is still a problem, go back with one or two others who feel the same way. If the person still refuses to listen or make any changes, take the matter to the church leaders. Christians who are not repentant should not be treated as though everything is all right. They need to be warned of the consequences of their continued sin. However, if the person chooses to repent, forgiveness and comfort are in order. Don't shut out someone who is genuinely repentant. Remember that the goal of discipline is not to judge or condemn but to correct and reconcile so everyone can live in harmony. As difficult as this may be, it is better than the alternatives: cutting off the relationship altogether due to anger or resentment, seeking revenge, or gossiping about the other person's sin. None of these results are healthy for individuals or for the greater community.

DIVINE PROMISE

MY CHILD, DON'T REJECT THE LORD'S
DISCIPLINE. . . . FOR THE LORD CORRECTS
THOSE HE LOVES. *Proverbs 3:11-12*

Discontent

MY QUESTION *for* GOD

How do I manage feelings of discontent?

A MOMENT *with* GOD

This same God who takes care of me will supply all your needs from his glorious riches, which have been given to us in Christ Jesus.   PHILIPPIANS 4:19

I will be your God throughout your lifetime—until your hair is white with age. I made you, and I will care for you.   ISAIAH 46:4

The LORD is my shepherd; I have all that I need.

PSALM 23:1

Seek the Kingdom of God above all else, and live righteously, and he will give you everything you need.   MATTHEW 6:33

God will generously provide all you need. Then you will always have everything you need and plenty left over to share with others.   2 CORINTHIANS 9:8

All humans have basic needs that must be met in order to survive: food, water, shelter, and love. However, our *needs* are different from our *wants*. When our needs are met, we can be content and satisfied. But our wants, even when they are fulfilled, can often leave us unsatisfied, discontent, and desiring more. Wants are not always negative, but when they are different from

God's desires, they can feed the fires of jealousy, covet-
ousness, deceit, materialism, or other sins we fall into
when we become obsessed with getting what we want.
Our needs often allow God to show us his power and
provision and teach us that he is sufficient. Our wants
often keep us from desiring and receiving God's help
because we're too focused on our own goals.

It is essential for a leader to recognize and manage the differences between needs and wants. As you
focus on meeting needs, you will learn to rely on God's
power, and you will begin to feel overall contentment.
But if you are feeling generally discontented, it may
be a sign that you are focusing too much on what you
want, which will never truly satisfy you. Focus instead
on discovering what God knows that you need. The
more you focus on what the Lord values, the more you
will be able to distinguish your wants from your needs.
Turn your feelings of discontent into a divine moment,
shifting your focus to the God who meets the needs
that truly satisfy.

DIVINE PROMISE

BY HIS DIVINE POWER, GOD HAS GIVEN US
EVERYTHING WE NEED FOR LIVING A GODLY
LIFE. WE HAVE RECEIVED ALL OF THIS BY
COMING TO KNOW HIM, THE ONE WHO
CALLED US TO HIMSELF BY MEANS OF HIS
MARVELOUS GLORY AND EXCELLENCE.   *2 Peter 1:3*

Discouragement

MY QUESTION *for* GOD

How should I respond to feelings of discouragement?

A MOMENT *with* GOD

Elijah was afraid and fled for his life. . . . "I have had enough, LORD," he said. "Take my life, for I am no better than my ancestors who have already died."

1 KINGS 19:3-4

Why am I discouraged? Why is my heart so sad? I will put my hope in God! I will praise him again—my Savior and my God! Now I am deeply discouraged, but I will remember you. . . . Each day the LORD pours his unfailing love upon me, and through each night I sing his songs, praying to God who gives me life. . . . Why am I discouraged? Why is my heart so sad? I will put my hope in God! I will praise him again—my Savior and my God!   PSALM 42:5-6, 8, 11

As soon as I pray, you answer me; you encourage me by giving me strength.   PSALM 138:3

From the depths of despair, O LORD, I call for your help.   PSALM 130:1

Discouragement often settles in when you are facing a problem or task that seems overwhelming, if not impossible; when you've really messed up and feel embarrassed or ashamed; when you work your hardest and still fail; when important relationships become strained; when you have expectations for greatness, but your limitations won't let you achieve it. Many people in the Bible faced discouragement. Elijah was deeply discouraged when he was the last prophet in Israel and his life was threatened. When you are discouraged, you feel like giving up—on God, friends, family, career, even hope itself. You feel like everyone is against you and nobody cares. What was most important to you now seems trivial. Worst of all, you can't see the way back to joy and happiness. When you reach your lowest point, you must determine whether you will sink deeper into the mire or begin to climb your way up and out of the pit. The opposite of discouragement is encouragement, and it is the antidote you need when you are down. God is your greatest encourager. Seek his help first, and then begin to praise him. Focusing on the character of God and everything he has already done for you will lift your spirits and help you overcome your discouragement.

DIVINE PROMISE

THE LORD IS CLOSE TO THE BROKENHEARTED;
HE RESCUES THOSE WHOSE SPIRITS ARE
CRUSHED. *Psalm 34:18*

Distractions

MY QUESTION *for* GOD

How can I deal with distractions?

A MOMENT *with* GOD

One day some parents brought their children to Jesus
so he could lay his hands on them and pray for them.
But the disciples scolded the parents for bothering
him. But Jesus said, "Let the children come to me.
Don't stop them! For the Kingdom of Heaven belongs
to those who are like these children." And he placed
his hands on their heads and blessed them before
he left.   MATTHEW 19:13-15

As Jesus was starting out on his way to Jerusalem,
a man came running up to him, knelt down, and
asked, "Good Teacher, what must I do to inherit
eternal life?"   MARK 10:17

*D*istractions bombarded Jesus all the time. But he
didn't see them as interruptions; he saw them as opportunities to save the lost or help someone in need.
When someone needs your help, a distraction can become a divine moment to show that person the love and
care of God. Sometimes God interrupts you for a good
reason. Don't miss the opportunity to serve the people
he brings to you for help.

The jailer called for lights and ran to the dungeon and
fell down trembling before Paul and Silas. Then he
brought them out and asked, "Sirs, what must I do to
be saved?" They replied, "Believe in the Lord Jesus
and you will be saved, along with everyone in your
household." And they shared the word of the Lord
with him.   ACTS 16:29-32

$\mathscr{M}$ost people would look at a jail sentence as a definite distraction from serving God. Not Paul and Silas! Their situation didn't stop them from their mission. Their ministry had taken them all over the ancient world, but it became confined to a small room with a very small audience. God seemed to be just fine with that. Instead of resisting the distraction, Paul and Silas embraced it. Sometimes a distraction seems as restricting as a jail cell. When that happens, maybe God wants you to focus on what and who is right in front of you. The distraction may be a call from God to minister to new people in a new way.

DIVINE PROMISE

I WILL TEACH YOU WISDOM'S WAYS AND LEAD
YOU IN STRAIGHT PATHS. WHEN YOU WALK,
YOU WON'T BE HELD BACK; WHEN YOU RUN,
YOU WON'T STUMBLE. *Proverbs 4:11-12*

$\mathscr{D}oubt$

MY QUESTION *for* GOD

Is it a sin to doubt God?

A MOMENT *with* GOD

When doubts filled my mind, your comfort gave me renewed hope and cheer. PSALM 94:19

John the Baptist, who was in prison, heard about all the things the Messiah was doing. So he sent his disciples to ask Jesus, "Are you the Messiah we've been expecting, or should we keep looking for someone else?"   MATTHEW 11:2-3

Jesus immediately reached out and grabbed [Peter]. "You have so little faith," Jesus said. "Why did you doubt me?"   MATTHEW 14:31

David, John the Baptist, Peter—all of them, along with many other biblical leaders, struggled with doubts about God and God's ability or desire to help them. This doesn't mean they had less faith, but their faith was challenged. God doesn't mind if you doubt him as long as you seek answers from him in the midst of your doubt. Doubt can become sin if it leads you away from God and into skepticism, cynicism, or hard-hearted-ness. But doubt can be beneficial when your honest searching leads you to a better understanding of God and deepens your faith in him. When you have moments of doubt, it's probably because you are in new territory. Allow your doubts to move you closer to God, not farther away from him.

DIVINE PROMISE

GOD HAS SAID, "I WILL NEVER FAIL YOU. I WILL NEVER ABANDON YOU." *Hebrews 13:5*

Doubt

MY QUESTION *for* GOD

How does overcoming doubt strengthen my faith?

A MOMENT *with* GOD

The LORD said to Gideon, "You have too many warriors with you. If I let all of you fight the Midianites, the Israelites will boast to me that they saved themselves by their own strength. Therefore, tell the people, 'Whoever is timid or afraid may leave this mountain and go home.'" So 22,000 of them went home, leaving only 10,000 who were willing to fight. But the LORD told Gideon, "There are still too many! Bring them down to the spring, and I will test them to determine who will go with you and who will not."

JUDGES 7:2-4

Doubt can be a trapdoor to fear, or it can be a doorway to confident faith. You may have doubts about God's ability to help you in the face of great odds, but you decide to trust him anyway. And when he acts, your faith is strengthened. God wants you to express your faith in him *before* he acts. So when God calls you to do something, don't be surprised if it seems that the obstacles are too great, as with Gideon when he faced the Midianites. This may be a test of your faith. God may be working to deepen your faith and character so you know it is really God who saves you, not your own efforts. As Gideon's army dwindled, he realized he was no longer in charge—only God could help him now. When you are humble enough to realize that you can't accomplish the job on your own, when you are ready to give God the credit rather than yourself, when you courageously hold on to your faith even if God calls you to do something that seems impossible—then you are in a position to see God at work, and your faith will be strengthened.

DIVINE PROMISE

WHEN DOUBTS FILLED MY MIND,
YOUR COMFORT GAVE ME RENEWED HOPE
AND CHEER. *Psalm 94:19*

Effectiveness

MY QUESTION *for* GOD

How can I improve my effectiveness on the job?

A MOMENT *with* GOD

Then the LORD said to Moses and Aaron, "Record the names of the members of the clans and families of the Kohathite division of the tribe of Levi. List all the men between the ages of thirty and fifty who are eligible to serve in the Tabernacle. The duties of the Kohathites at the Tabernacle will relate to the most sacred objects. When the camp moves, Aaron and his sons must enter the Tabernacle first to take down the inner curtain. . . . Next they must spread a blue cloth over the table. . . . Next they must cover the lampstand. . . . They must remove the ashes

from the altar. . . . Aaron and his sons will direct
the Gershonites regarding all their duties, whether it
involves moving the equipment or doing other work.
. . . [The Merarites'] only duty at the Tabernacle will
be to carry loads. They will carry the frames of the
Tabernacle, the crossbars, the posts, and the bases.

NUMBERS 4:1-5, 7, 9, 13, 27, 31

*W*hat if God had simply told the Levites to find something to do around the Tabernacle? Not much work
would have been accomplished! Instead, God organized
the Levites into teams with specific responsibilities.
This can teach us important principles about effectiveness. Organizing, planning, and delegating are key elements of effectiveness. Rather than inhibit us, these
steps free us to be more productive and useful. Having the Tabernacle duties clearly assigned freed up the
Levites to focus on ministering to people. Sometimes
we need to slow down in order to speed up. When you
pause to organize your work, you can move ahead more
effectively as you serve God.

DIVINE PROMISE

TO THOSE WHO USE WELL WHAT THEY ARE
GIVEN, EVEN MORE WILL BE GIVEN. *Matthew 25:29*

Emptiness

MY QUESTIONS *for* GOD

Why do I feel so empty? How do I fill the emptiness inside me?

A MOMENT *with* GOD

When an evil spirit leaves a person, it goes into the desert, searching for rest. But when it finds none, it says, "I will return to the person I came from." So it returns and finds that its former home is all swept and in order. Then the spirit finds seven other spirits more evil than itself, and they all enter the person and live there. And so that person is worse off than before.   LUKE 11:24-26

Let them no longer fool themselves by trusting in empty riches, for emptiness will be their only reward.   JOB 15:31

May you experience the love of Christ, though it is too great to understand fully. Then you will be made complete with all the fullness of life and power that comes from God.   EPHESIANS 3:19

Jesus replied, "Anyone who drinks this water will soon become thirsty again. But those who drink the water I give will never be thirsty again. It becomes a fresh, bubbling spring within them, giving them eternal life."   JOHN 4:13-14

When something is empty, either it no longer works or it no longer satisfies. But when *someone* is empty, there is no longer any motivation, meaning, or purpose. There seems to be no reason to go on. Many things can cause you to feel empty—the death of a loved one, the end of a friendship, being ignored or rejected. Feelings of emptiness often follow some kind of loss. Loss empties your emotional tank and uses up all your reserves. It leaves you hungry and thirsty, looking for something to fill and satisfy the emptiness. This is the moment Satan has been waiting for. He is always ready to move in to an empty heart. He tries to deceive you into thinking that what he offers can satisfy you. But only God can fill the emptiness inside you and satisfy your deepest needs. When your heart is filled with the love, truth, and goodness of God, there is no room for evil to enter. It is only through the presence of God's Spirit within you that meaning, purpose, and satisfaction will be restored. God created you to be truly fulfilled when you fill your soul with him.

DIVINE PROMISE

I PRAY THAT GOD, THE SOURCE OF HOPE, WILL FILL YOU COMPLETELY WITH JOY AND PEACE BECAUSE YOU TRUST IN HIM. THEN YOU WILL OVERFLOW WITH CONFIDENT HOPE THROUGH THE POWER OF THE HOLY SPIRIT. *Romans 15:13*

Emptiness

MY QUESTION *for* GOD

I'm so busy doing things, but I still feel empty. Where does this emptiness come from?

A MOMENT *with* GOD

I will wound you! I will bring you to ruin for all your sins. You will eat but never have enough. Your hunger pangs and emptiness will remain. And though you try to save your money, it will come to nothing in the end.   MICAH 6:13-14

One of sin's great deceptions is that more will be enough, but it never is. If you always think you need just a little more to satisfy you, then you will never be satisfied.

Wherever your treasure is, there the desires of your heart will also be.   MATTHEW 6:21

Feelings of emptiness can come when your heart is not filled up enough with God. Often this happens when something else becomes more important to you than God. God created you to have a relationship with him. When you push the Creator into a corner of your heart or push him out entirely, you leave a big hole. A heart without God is an empty heart.

We are merely moving shadows, and all our busy rushing ends in nothing. We heap up wealth, not knowing who will spend it.   PSALM 39:6

Feelings of emptiness can come when you confuse accomplishment with purpose. You may do a lot and seem to accomplish much; but if there is no eternal purpose behind your work, after a while it all feels empty and meaningless.

If I gave everything I have to the poor and even sacrificed my body, I could boast about it; but if I didn't love others, I would have gained nothing.

1 CORINTHIANS 13:3

Feelings of emptiness can come from living without loving. Without love, we can gain nothing from all our efforts.

Let them no longer fool themselves by trusting in empty riches, for emptiness will be their only reward.

JOB 15:31

Feelings of emptiness can come when your main focus is accumulating wealth. Eventually you realize that it doesn't really satisfy as you thought it would, and you can't take it with you when you die.

Unless the LORD builds a house, the work of the builders is wasted. Unless the LORD protects a city, guarding it with sentries will do no good. It is useless for you to work so hard from early morning until late at night, anxiously working for food to eat; for God gives rest to his loved ones.

PSALM 127:1-2

Feelings of emptiness can come when you seek satisfaction only in your work. Work can satisfy and fulfill you for a time, but even rewarding work cannot ultimately satisfy. One day you will no longer work, and then what will satisfy? Retirement? When you are too old to enjoy that, then what will satisfy?

So, my dear brothers and sisters, be strong and immovable. Always work enthusiastically for the Lord, for you know that nothing you do for the Lord is ever useless.   1 CORINTHIANS 15:58

Feelings of emptiness fade away when you find meaning and purpose in life and when God uses you to accomplish the purpose for which he created you.

DIVINE PROMISE
THE THIEF'S PURPOSE IS TO STEAL AND KILL
AND DESTROY. MY PURPOSE IS TO GIVE THEM
A RICH AND SATISFYING LIFE. *John 10:10*

Encouragement

MY QUESTION *for* GOD
How can I be an encouragement to those I lead?

A MOMENT *with* GOD
Jonathan went to find David and encouraged him to
stay strong in his faith in God.   1 SAMUEL 23:16

*T*hrough your words and your example, you can encourage others to stay close to God.

Don't use foul or abusive language. Let everything you say be good and helpful, so that your words will be an encouragement to those who hear them.

EPHESIANS 4:29

*D*etermine that your words will always be positive, wholesome, helpful, and encouraging to those you lead.

He must have a strong belief in the trustworthy message he was taught; then he will be able to encourage others with wholesome teaching and show those who oppose it where they are wrong.   TITUS 1:9

*S*hare with others what you have learned from God's Word.

A cheerful look brings joy to the heart; good news makes for good health.   PROVERBS 15:30

*S*mile at people!

Haggai and Zechariah son of Iddo prophesied to the Jews in Judah and Jerusalem. They prophesied in the name of the God of Israel who was over them. Zerubbabel son of Shealtiel and Jeshua son of Jehozadak responded by starting again to rebuild the Temple of God in Jerusalem. And the prophets of God were with them and helped them.   EZRA 5:1-2

*E*ncourage people to get involved in serving God in some practical way.

Now he is very useful to both of us.   PHILEMON 1:11

*S*how others you trust them enough to give them important tasks.

I recall all you have done, O LORD; I remember your wonderful deeds of long ago.   PSALM 77:11

*R*eview with others the ways God has worked in your lives and blessed you in the past.

"He may have a great army, but they are merely men. We have the LORD our God to help us and to fight our battles for us!" Hezekiah's words greatly encouraged the people.   2 CHRONICLES 32:8

I am certain that God, who began the good work within you, will continue his work until it is finally finished.   PHILIPPIANS 1:6

*R*emind others of what God wants to do for them and through them.

Hezekiah encouraged all the Levites regarding the skill they displayed as they served the LORD.

2 CHRONICLES 30:22

Compliment people for a job well done.

[Barnabas] encouraged the believers to stay true to
the Lord.   ACTS 11:23

Encourage the people you lead to hold fast to godly
principles and to live their faith. Barnabas, whose name
means "son of encouragement," brought many people
to faith in the Lord through his words and faithful
example.

DIVINE CHALLENGE

ENCOURAGE EACH OTHER AND BUILD EACH
OTHER UP, JUST AS YOU ARE ALREADY DOING.
1 Thessalonians 5:11

Endurance

MY QUESTION *for* GOD

How can I be a good leader over the long haul?

A MOMENT *with* GOD

Are you seeking great things for yourself? Don't do
it! I will bring great disaster upon all these people;
but I will give you your life as a reward wherever you
go. I, the LORD, have spoken!   JEREMIAH 45:5

The greatest among you must be a servant.

MATTHEW 23:11

$\mathscr{I}$t is certainly difficult to keep doing well over a long period of time, especially when life throws you trials and temptations. A leader who has an enduring faith, however, is up to the challenge. The ability to be steady for the long-term is born out of godly motives. On the other hand, the desire for status, control, or acceptance is not an adequate motive for leadership that endures. You will inevitably be disappointed, for Jesus promises you none of these things. In fact, Jesus taught that whoever wants to be the greatest must be willing to be the least and serve everyone else. You should serve because you love God and you love others in his name. This will not make leadership easy, but it will enable you to endure as you find deep joy in serving others.

DIVINE CHALLENGE

LET'S NOT GET TIRED OF DOING WHAT IS GOOD. AT JUST THE RIGHT TIME WE WILL REAP A HARVEST OF BLESSING IF WE DON'T GIVE UP.

Galatians 6:9

$\mathscr{E}nemies$

MY QUESTION *for* GOD

Who are my enemies, and how can they defeat me?

A MOMENT *with* GOD

Then Delilah pouted, "How can you tell me, 'I love you,' when you don't share your secrets with me? . . ."

She tormented him with her nagging day after day
until he was sick to death of it. Finally, Samson shared
his secret with her. . . . The Philistines captured him
and . . . he was bound with bronze chains.

JUDGES 16:15-17, 21

Stay alert! Watch out for your great enemy, the devil.
He prowls around like a roaring lion, looking for
someone to devour. Stand firm against him, and be
strong in your faith. 1 PETER 5:8-9

Put on every piece of God's armor so you will be able
to resist the enemy in the time of evil. Then after the
battle you will still be standing firm. EPHESIANS 6:13

*T*emptation is an enemy that always strikes at your
weak spot. The Philistines knew they couldn't match
Samson's brute strength, so they aimed at his weakness—his inability to stay away from seductive women.
"How can you say you love me?" Delilah whined.
And Samson gave in. Your weak spots are those areas you refuse to give over to God, the areas in which
you compromise your convictions for a few moments
of pleasure. They are joints in your spiritual armor,
and the enemy takes aim at them. It is in those areas
of weakness where you must ask God for help so he
can protect your vulnerable spots with his strength.
Your own weaknesses can become your enemy. You
must understand them so you can arm yourself against
Satan's attacks. It is disastrous to discover your weak
spots in the heat of the battle, as Samson did. Then it

is too late, and the enemy will defeat you. You must discover your weaknesses before the fighting begins. With the Lord fighting beside you and with a strategy in place to protect your most vulnerable points, you will be prepared for any enemy.

DIVINE PROMISE

BE STRONG IN THE LORD AND IN HIS MIGHTY POWER. PUT ON ALL OF GOD'S ARMOR SO THAT YOU WILL BE ABLE TO STAND FIRM AGAINST ALL STRATEGIES OF THE DEVIL. *Ephesians 6:10-11*

Energy

MY QUESTION *for* GOD

How can I have more energy?

A MOMENT *with* GOD

Work with enthusiasm, as though you were working for the Lord rather than for people.   EPHESIANS 6:7

*W*hen you do your work as though you were doing it for the Lord, you can work with more enthusiasm and energy. When you work to please the Lord and not just people, your efforts will be more rewarding and energizing.

Let's not get tired of doing what is good. At just the right time we will reap a harvest of blessing if we don't give up. GALATIANS 6:9

*R*ealizing that God will reward your efforts helps you work with sustained energy.

No, dear brothers and sisters, I have not achieved it, but I focus on this one thing: Forgetting the past and looking forward to what lies ahead. PHILIPPIANS 3:13

*Y*ou will have more energy for today and tomorrow if you don't waste it focusing on yesterday.

Using a dull ax requires great strength, so sharpen the blade. That's the value of wisdom; it helps you succeed. ECCLESIASTES 10:10

*W*isdom gives you energy because it provides you with discernment and a deeper perspective on your work.

"This is not good!" Moses' father-in-law exclaimed. "You're going to wear yourself out—and the people, too. . . . Let me give you a word of advice, and may God be with you. . . . Select from all the people some capable, honest men who fear God and hate bribes. Appoint them as leaders over groups of one thousand, one hundred, fifty, and ten. They should always be available to solve the people's common disputes, but have them bring the major cases to you. Let

the leaders decide the smaller matters themselves.
They will help you carry the load, making the task
easier for you. If you follow this advice, and if God
commands you to do so, then you will be able to
endure the pressures, and all these people will go
home in peace."   EXODUS 18:17-23

*D*elegating some tasks to others will lighten your load
and help you conserve energy. As an added benefit, the
job will be done more efficiently and effectively.

Remember to observe the Sabbath day by keeping it
holy. You have six days each week for your ordinary
work, but the seventh day is a Sabbath day of rest
dedicated to the LORD your God.   EXODUS 20:8-10

*S*etting aside times of rest renews you mentally, physically, emotionally, and physically. Taking a break gives
you more energy for the work ahead.

No discipline is enjoyable while it is happening—it's
painful! But afterward there will be a peaceful
harvest of right living for those who are trained in
this way. So take a new grip with your tired hands
and strengthen your weak knees.   HEBREWS 12:11-12

*W*hen you know you are doing the right thing, it can
rejuvenate you. You realize that God is pleased with
your actions, there is great energy in pleasing God.

EXAMPLE   131

That is why I tell you not to worry about everyday life—whether you have enough food and drink, or enough clothes to wear. Isn't life more than food, and your body more than clothing? Look at the birds. They don't plant or harvest or store food in barns, for your heavenly Father feeds them. And aren't you far more valuable to him than they are? Can all your worries add a single moment to your life?

MATTHEW 6:25-27

*W*orrying saps your energy, but trusting in God recharges and energizes you.

DIVINE PROMISE

HE GIVES POWER TO THE WEAK AND STRENGTH TO THE POWERLESS. EVEN YOUTHS WILL BECOME WEAK AND TIRED, AND YOUNG MEN WILL FALL IN EXHAUSTION. BUT THOSE WHO TRUST IN THE LORD WILL FIND NEW STRENGTH. THEY WILL SOAR HIGH ON WINGS LIKE EAGLES. THEY WILL RUN AND NOT GROW WEARY. THEY WILL WALK AND NOT FAINT.   *Isaiah 40:29-31*

Example

MY QUESTION *for* GOD

What qualities should I have to be a good example to others?

A Moment *with* God

Whoever wants to be a leader among you must be your servant.

NEHEMIAH 20:26

Then I pressed further, "What you are doing is not right!"

NEHEMIAH 5:9

He must become greater and greater, and I must become less and less.

JOHN 3:30

If you want those you lead to look up to you as a good example, then have a servant's heart, take responsibility for your actions, speak up when something is wrong, and do not seek glory for yourself. The world often teaches leaders to look and act cool, to use coarse or foul language, to disrespect other authority or abuse their own, and to bend the rules for themselves. But in the end, the people who consistently live with kindness, integrity, and a deep love for God will be the most respected and honored.

DIVINE PROMISE

I WILL GIVE YOU SHEPHERDS AFTER MY OWN HEART, WHO WILL GUIDE YOU WITH KNOWLEDGE AND UNDERSTANDING. *Jeremiah 3:15*

Excellence

MY QUESTIONS *for* GOD

Why does God encourage excellence? Should I strive for excellence?

A MOMENT *with* GOD

Do you have the gift of speaking? Then speak as though God himself were speaking through you.

1 PETER 4:11

I run with purpose in every step. I am not just shadowboxing.   1 CORINTHIANS 9:26

Imitate God, therefore, in everything you do.

EPHESIANS 5:1

Excellence means performing beyond expectations. An excellent car is not merely one that is bigger than other models but one that performs better, accomplishes its purposes better, and actually makes driving fun. Excellence also helps other people beyond their own expectations. A medical doctor who strives for excellence might develop a new vaccine that saves people's lives. God is the standard for excellence. No machine has ever been able to duplicate the marvelous complexity that God created in the human body. No artist can paint a picture that rivals a beautiful sunset in the real world. God wants you to pursue excellence because it shows that you care about doing things right, that you care about helping people to the best of your

ability, and that you care about modeling the characteristics of the God you worship and follow.

DIVINE PROMISE

WORK WILLINGLY AT WHATEVER YOU DO, AS
THOUGH YOU WERE WORKING FOR THE LORD
RATHER THAN FOR PEOPLE. REMEMBER THAT
THE LORD WILL GIVE YOU AN INHERITANCE AS
YOUR REWARD, AND THAT THE MASTER YOU
ARE SERVING IS CHRIST.   *Colossians 3:23-24*

Expectations

MY QUESTION *for* GOD

What does God expect of me?

A MOMENT *with* GOD

What does the LORD your God require of you? He
requires only that you fear the LORD your God,
and live in a way that pleases him, and love him and
serve him with all your heart and soul. And you must
always obey the LORD's commands and decrees that I
am giving you today for your own good.

DEUTERONOMY 10:12-13

*H*uman beings have always had a tendency to make
religion more complicated than it has to be, but God
clearly tells us what he expects of us. Moses concisely

summarizes the essential elements of a genuine relationship with God:

1. Fear. Have deep respect and reverence for God.
2. Obey. Live according to God's will by obeying his commands.
3. Worship. Express your love for God when you worship him with all your heart and soul.

Make sure each day includes these three elements, and your life will be pleasing to God and a wonderful example for others to follow.

DIVINE PROMISE

ALL PRAISE TO GOD, THE FATHER OF OUR LORD JESUS CHRIST. IT IS BY HIS GREAT MERCY THAT WE HAVE BEEN BORN AGAIN, BECAUSE GOD RAISED JESUS CHRIST FROM THE DEAD. NOW WE LIVE WITH GREAT EXPECTATION, AND WE HAVE A PRICELESS INHERITANCE— AN INHERITANCE THAT IS KEPT IN HEAVEN FOR YOU, PURE AND UNDEFILED, BEYOND THE REACH OF CHANGE AND DECAY. *1 Peter 1:3-4*

Experience

MY QUESTION *for* GOD

I'm an experienced leader, but I am no longer in a leadership position. I feel stuck on the shelf. What do I do?

A MOMENT *with* GOD

He took David from tending the ewes and lambs and made him the shepherd of Jacob's descendants—God's own people, Israel. He cared for them with a true heart and led them with skillful hands.

PSALM 78:71-72

*D*o your best wherever you are, and remember that God wastes nothing. Instead, God uses everything to further his good purposes. David's first job was shepherding—hardly the recommended grooming for a future king! Yet the lessons David learned on the hills with the sheep served him well on the throne. He ruled not as a tyrant but as a shepherd. God will use you in whatever situation you find yourself, and God will use your circumstances to prepare you for future service. If it feels like God has put you on the shelf, then grow and serve there. God's plan is still in action now, not just at some point in the future. Serving right where you are can be a divine moment of preparation for where God eventually wants to use you.

DIVINE PROMISE

I AM CERTAIN THAT GOD, WHO BEGAN THE GOOD WORK WITHIN YOU, WILL CONTINUE HIS WORK UNTIL IT IS FINALLY FINISHED ON THE DAY WHEN CHRIST JESUS RETURNS.

Philippians 1:6

Failure

MY QUESTION *for* GOD

How can God bring anything good out of failure?

A MOMENT *with* GOD

Now all glory to God, who is able to keep you from falling away and will bring you with great joy into his glorious presence without a single fault. All glory to him who alone is God, our Savior through Jesus Christ our Lord. All glory, majesty, power, and authority are his before all time, and in the present, and beyond all time!   JUDE 1:24-25

*T*rain yourself to live according to God's definition of failure and success. The world defines success as an abundance of achievements and possessions; it defines failure as a lack of those things. God defines success as obedience to him, which results in love for others, godly character, living with integrity, salvation, and eternal life in heaven. God defines failure as rejecting him. Live by God's definition of success, and your earthly failures will be only temporary.

DIVINE PROMISE

THE LORD DIRECTS THE STEPS OF THE GODLY. HE DELIGHTS IN EVERY DETAIL OF THEIR LIVES. THOUGH THEY STUMBLE, THEY WILL NEVER FALL, FOR THE LORD HOLDS THEM BY THE HAND.   *Psalm 37:23-24*

Faith

MY QUESTION *for* GOD

How does my faith affect the way I lead?

A MOMENT *with* GOD

The LORD had said to Abram, "Leave your native country." . . . So Abram departed as the LORD had instructed.   GENESIS 12:1, 4

Elisha prayed, "O LORD, open his eyes and let him see!" The LORD opened the young man's eyes, and when he looked up, he saw that the hillside around Elisha was filled with horses and chariots of fire.

2 KINGS 6:17

Whenever the cloud lifted from over the sacred tent, the people of Israel would break camp and follow it. And wherever the cloud settled, the people of Israel would set up camp.   NUMBERS 9:17

Trust in the LORD with all your heart; do not depend on your own understanding. Seek his will in all you do, and he will show you which path to take.

PROVERBS 3:5-6

Faith is more than just believing; it is staking our very lives on what we believe. For example, we may believe that someone can walk across a deep gorge on a tight-rope. But are we willing to trust that person to carry us? If you had faith, you would say yes. Faith in God means that we are willing to trust him with our very lives. We are willing to follow his guidelines for living, as outlined in the Bible, because we have the conviction that this is best for us. We are even willing to endure ridicule and persecution for our faith because we are so sure that God is who he says he is and will keep his promises about salvation and eternal life in heaven. Faith in God means he is our leader. Then when we are put into a leadership position, we must fight the temptation to be the final authority. We must not lead as though everything were depending on us or forget that we trust God to do the leading. Like a muscle, faith gets stronger the more you exercise it. Exercise your faith when you lead, or you may miss out on the exciting places God wants to take you.

DIVINE PROMISE

WHEN YOUR FAITH REMAINS STRONG
THROUGH MANY TRIALS, IT WILL BRING YOU
MUCH PRAISE AND GLORY AND HONOR ON
THE DAY WHEN JESUS CHRIST IS REVEALED TO
THE WHOLE WORLD.   *1 Peter 1:7*

Fasting

MY QUESTION *for* GOD

Why should I fast?

A MOMENT *with* GOD

Jehoshaphat was terrified by this news and begged the LORD for guidance. He also ordered everyone in Judah to begin fasting.   2 CHRONICLES 20:3

When this vision came to me, I, Daniel, had been in mourning for three whole weeks. All that time I had eaten no rich food. No meat or wine crossed my lips, and I used no fragrant lotions.   DANIEL 10:2-3

Jesus, full of the Holy Spirit, returned from the Jordan River. He was led by the Spirit in the wilderness, where he was tempted by the devil for forty days. Jesus ate nothing all that time and became very hungry. . . . Then Jesus returned to Galilee, filled with the Holy Spirit's power.   LUKE 4:1-2, 14

Paul and Barnabas also appointed elders in every church. With prayer and fasting, they turned the elders over to the care of the Lord, in whom they had put their trust.   ACTS 14:23

*Sometimes we talk with our hands to better express what we are trying to communicate. Our gestures add a more tangible passion, emphasis, or elaboration to our words. Fasting is similar—it's a more tangible way of communicating with God. Some have said that fasting is praying with the body. It is one thing to talk to God, to tell him you love him, to ask him to talk to you. But sometimes it helps to *do* something as you communicate with God; it can add more focus, commitment, and passion to your conversation with him. Most of us think of fasting as *not* doing something, such as not eating. But fasting really is *doing* something. It involves taking specific steps to temporarily alter a daily habit. The act of stopping something you normally do often takes more effort than just continuing to do it.

When you fast, you are stopping one thing in order to more fully focus on something else, namely, communicating with God. Fasting is making the extra effort to tell God you are serious about what he has to say. It sharpens your mind and allows you to be more receptive to what God has to say. Perhaps most important, fasting is one way emphasize to God just how much you value your communication with him.

DIVINE PROMISE

WHEN YOU FAST, DON'T MAKE IT OBVIOUS. . . .
THEN NO ONE WILL NOTICE THAT YOU ARE
FASTING, EXCEPT YOUR FATHER, WHO KNOWS
WHAT YOU DO IN PRIVATE. AND YOUR FATHER,
WHO SEES EVERYTHING, WILL REWARD YOU.
Matthew 6:16-18

Fear

MY QUESTION *for* GOD

What do I do when I feel paralyzed by fear?

A MOMENT *with* GOD

This was their report to Moses: "We entered the land you sent us to explore, and it is indeed a bountiful country—a land flowing with milk and honey. Here is the kind of fruit it produces. But the people living there are powerful, and their towns are large and fortified. We even saw giants there. . . . But Caleb

tried to quiet the people as they stood before Moses.
"Let's go at once to take the land," he said. "We can
certainly conquer it!" But the other men who had
explored the land with him disagreed. "We can't go
up against them! They are stronger than we are!"

NUMBERS 13:27-31

Fear is real, and fear is normal—but it can paralyze
us. When the Israelite spies returned from scouting out
the Promised Land, they faced an issue of reality versus
distortion. The reality was that God had already promised that the Israelite people would conquer the land (see
Exodus 3:8; Leviticus 20:24). The fact that God himself
ordered the scouts into the land should have given them
great confidence. The distortion of reality came from
the giants that seemed bigger and more immediate than
God's promise. Fear can distort your view of reality.
It makes the giants in your path appear more powerful
than your almighty God, who promises to deliver you.
Sooner or later you will face fearsome giants in your
life—an especially great temptation, guilt, sin, anger,
anxiety, depression, or something else. Don't let the size
of the giant reduce the size of your God!

DIVINE PROMISE

I HOLD YOU BY YOUR RIGHT HAND—I, THE
LORD YOUR GOD. AND I SAY TO YOU, "DON'T BE
AFRAID. I AM HERE TO HELP YOU." *Isaiah 41:13*

Fellowship

MY QUESTION *for* GOD

How is Christian fellowship different from other kinds of friendship?

A MOMENT *with* GOD

When we get together, I want to encourage you in your faith, but I also want to be encouraged by yours.

ROMANS 1:12

Confess your sins to each other and pray for each other so that you may be healed.   JAMES 5:16

[Jesus said,] "Where two or three gather together as my followers, I am there among them."   MATTHEW 18:20

Good friends are a wonderful gift, but fellowship among believers in Jesus (such as the kind of fellowship you find at church or in small-group ministries) is unique because it invites the living God into your midst. Christians have a common perspective on life because they know their sins have been forgiven, they have experienced the joy of salvation, and they know they have a future together in heaven. Christian fellowship provides a place for honest sharing about the things that really matter in life. It provides encouragement to stay strong in the face of temptation and persecution, and it offers supernatural help in dealing with problems. Christian leaders need Christian fellowship so they can stand strong in their convictions, lead with

integrity, and be encouraged that their desire for truth
will be rewarded by God.

DIVINE PROMISE

IF WE ARE LIVING IN THE LIGHT, AS GOD IS IN
THE LIGHT, THEN WE HAVE FELLOWSHIP WITH
EACH OTHER, AND THE BLOOD OF JESUS, HIS
SON, CLEANSES US FROM ALL SIN.   *1 John 1:7*

Finishing

MY QUESTION *for* GOD

What can inspire me to finish well?

A MOMENT *with* GOD

The years passed, and the LORD had given the people
of Israel rest from all their enemies. Joshua, who was
now very old, called together all the elders, leaders,
judges, and officers of Israel. He said to them, "I am
now a very old man. You have seen everything the
LORD your God has done for you during my lifetime.
The LORD your God has fought for you against your
enemies. . . . So be very careful to follow everything
Moses wrote in the Book of Instruction. Do not
deviate from it, turning either to the right or to the
left. . . . Cling tightly to the LORD your God as you
have done until now."   JOSHUA 23:1-3, 6-8

As the years take a toll on our bodies, it may be painful to realize we no longer possess the physical skills or energy we used to have. As old age settles upon us, the wrinkles, aches, and pains make us realize that our lives are nearing their final chapters. How sad when others dismiss older people, as though their earthly contributions are finished! Joshua, as an old man, demonstrated that older believers can be a powerful witness to the constant mercy and faithfulness of God. There are few things more powerful than the testimony of someone who has lived a long life of faithfulness to the Lord and still maintains the vibrant vision of an eternal God who keeps his promises. As you grow older in the faith, younger people who listen to your life story will be greatly impacted by God's faithfulness to you through the decades. If you are still a young leader, find an older believer and ask him or her to tell you about God's faithfulness in his or her life. Be prepared to hear some amazing stories! If you are already older, commit yourself to finishing well. When you demonstrate faithfulness to God to the end, the telling of your story will be a divine moment in the lives of those who hear it.

DIVINE PROMISE

I AM CERTAIN THAT GOD, WHO BEGAN THE GOOD WORK WITHIN YOU, WILL CONTINUE HIS WORK UNTIL IT IS FINALLY FINISHED ON THE DAY WHEN CHRIST JESUS RETURNS.

Philippians 1:6

Flexibility

MY QUESTION *for* GOD

How can I be more flexible when God calls me to do something?

A MOMENT *with* GOD

A Jewish man was traveling on a trip . . . and he
was attacked by bandits. They . . . beat him up, and
left him half dead beside the road. . . . A despised
Samaritan came along, and when he saw the man,
he felt compassion for him. Going over to him, the
Samaritan soothed his wounds with olive oil and wine
and bandaged them. Then he put the man on his own
donkey and took him to an inn, where he took care
of him.   LUKE 10:30, 33-34

Be willing to adapt your schedule to respond to someone in need.

All Scripture is inspired by God and is useful to teach
us what is true and to make us realize what is wrong
in our lives. It corrects us when we are wrong and
teaches us to do what is right. God uses it to prepare
and equip his people to do every good work.

                                          2 TIMOTHY 3:16-17

Use God's Word and prayer as the tools to prepare
you for what God has in store for you. They also prepare you to adapt to life's changes, when trials and cri-
ses come your way.

I heard the LORD asking, "Whom should I send as a messenger to this people? Who will go for us?" I said, "Here I am. Send me."

ISAIAH 6:8

*L*isten for, recognize, and willingly respond to God's voice in your life.

Mary responded, "I am the Lord's servant. May everything you have said about me come true." And then the angel left her.

LUKE 1:38

*B*e willing to be used by God whenever he calls and for whatever tasks he calls you to do.

The LORD spoke to Jonah a second time: "Get up and go to the great city of Nineveh, and deliver the message I have given you." This time Jonah obeyed the LORD's command and went to Nineveh.

JONAH 3:1-3

*B*e obedient to God every day. Whether or not he calls you to do something else, you will already be doing his will and following his call.

DIVINE PROMISE

THE WISDOM FROM ABOVE IS FIRST OF ALL PURE. IT IS ALSO PEACE LOVING, GENTLE AT ALL TIMES, AND WILLING TO YIELD TO OTHERS.

James 3:17

Forgiveness

MY QUESTION *for* GOD

Why is forgiveness an important concept for leaders?

A MOMENT *with* GOD

Make allowance for each other's faults, and forgive
anyone who offends you. Remember, the Lord
forgave you, so you must forgive others. COLOSSIANS 3:13

Don't repay evil for evil. Don't retaliate with insults
when people insult you. Instead, pay them back with
a blessing. That is what God has called you to do, and
he will bless you for it.   1 PETER 3:9

If you forgive those who sin against you, your
heavenly Father will forgive you. But if you refuse to
forgive others, your Father will not forgive your sins.
                                              MATTHEW 6:14-15

The stress and tensions of leadership and interper-
sonal relationships mean there will be frequent conflicts and friction between leaders and those they lead.
Wise leaders make candid confession and forgiveness
a way of life for their groups or organizations. You are
in a position to set the tone, among believers and nonbelievers alike. You should be motivated by the clear
teaching of God's Word that you will receive God's
forgiveness only when you are willing to forgive those
who have wronged you.

When you are praying, first forgive anyone you are holding a grudge against, so that your Father in heaven will forgive your sins, too.   MARK 11:25

Watch yourselves! If another believer sins, rebuke that person; then if there is repentance, forgive. Even if that person wrongs you seven times a day and each time turns again and asks forgiveness, you must forgive.   LUKE 17:3-4

Peter came to him and asked, "Lord, how often should I forgive someone who sins against me? Seven times?" "No, not seven times," Jesus replied, "but seventy times seven!"   MATTHEW 18:21-22

*J*ust as God forgives you without limit, you should forgive others without keeping track.

I am not overstating it when I say that the man who caused all the trouble hurt all of you more than he hurt me. Most of you opposed him, and that was punishment enough. Now, however, it is time to forgive and comfort him. Otherwise he may be overcome by discouragement. So I urge you now to reaffirm your love for him.   2 CORINTHIANS 2:5-8

*L*eaders should understand that refusing to forgive a person can lead to serious and harmful consequences for the offender. It is acceptable to require a person to suffer natural and logical consequences for their

mistakes or offenses, but do not discourage them by
withholding forgiveness.

Divine Challenge

MAKE ALLOWANCE FOR EACH OTHER'S FAULTS,
AND FORGIVE ANYONE WHO OFFENDS YOU.
REMEMBER, THE LORD FORGAVE YOU, SO YOU
MUST FORGIVE OTHERS.   *Colossians 3:13*

Future

My Question *for* God

*I'm afraid that trusting God means he will lead me where I
don't want to go. How can I stop worrying about the future?*

A Moment *with* God

Take delight in the LORD, and he will give you your
heart's desires.   PSALM 37:4

My purpose is to give them a rich and satisfying life.

JOHN 10:10

May he grant your heart's desires and make all your
plans succeed.   PSALM 20:4

"I know the plans I have for you," says the LORD.
"They are plans for good and not for disaster, to give
you a future and a hope."   JEREMIAH 29:11

God's plans are always good. His desires for you will fulfill and satisfy you. If your mind and heart are truly in tune with God's will, you'll never be led where you don't want to go. God changes your heart before he adjusts your plans for the future. Let him change your heart. Since God alone knows the future, no one can plan for it better than he.

DIVINE PROMISE

HE FILLS MY LIFE WITH GOOD THINGS.
Psalm 103:5

Goals

MY QUESTION *for* GOD

Why is it important to have goals?

A MOMENT *with* GOD

The LORD had said to Abram, "Leave your native country, your relatives, and your father's family, and go to the land that I will show you. I will make you into a great nation. I will bless you and make you famous, and you will be a blessing to others. I will bless those who bless you and curse those who treat you with contempt. All the families on earth will be blessed through you." So Abram departed as the LORD had instructed.   GENESIS 12:1-4

God's goals for you should determine your personal goals and set the agenda for your life. God's promise to Abram gave him such a strong purpose and direction that he risked everything to pursue it.

I run with purpose in every step. I am not just shadowboxing. I discipline my body like an athlete, training it to do what it should.   1 CORINTHIANS 9:26-27

Goals keep you focused on your primary mission and determine how you conduct your life. They shape the way you live each day and guide your interaction with others.

I don't have the strength to endure. I have nothing to live for.   JOB 6:11

Goals give you strength and endurance and something to live for.

Either way, Christ's love controls us.

2 CORINTHIANS 5:14

Let's not get tired of doing what is good. At just the right time we will reap a harvest of blessing if we don't give up.   GALATIANS 6:9

Goals motivate us, energize us, and bring us hope.

All of you should be of one mind. Sympathize with each other. Love each other as brothers and sisters. Be tenderhearted, and keep a humble attitude. Don't repay evil for evil. Don't retaliate with insults when people insult you. Instead, pay them back with a blessing. That is what God has called you to do, and he will bless you for it.   1 PETER 3:8-9

𝒢oals can be rewarding when they help and bless others.

Look straight ahead, and fix your eyes on what lies before you. Mark out a straight path for your feet; stay on the safe path. Don't get sidetracked; keep your feet from following evil.   PROVERBS 4:25-27

𝒢oals keep you focused on godly pursuits so that you aren't distracted by temptation.

I brought glory to you here on earth by completing the work you gave me to do.   JOHN 17:4

𝒢oals keep you from doing too much. God is glorified not when you do everything you possibly can do but rather when you fulfill the goals he has for you.

David said, "This will be the location for the Temple of the LORD God and the place of the altar for Israel's burnt offerings!" So David gave orders to call together the foreigners living in Israel, and he

assigned them the task of preparing finished stone for
building the Temple of God. . . . David said, . . . "I
will begin making preparations for it now." So David
collected vast amounts of building materials before
his death.   1 CHRONICLES 22:1-2, 5

*G*oals that are inspired by a leader's bold vision can
help everyone accomplish great things. David's vision
for the Temple was fulfilled through the work of many
people coming together to build a magnificent structure for the glory of God.

DIVINE PROMISE

I HAVE NOT ACHIEVED IT, BUT I FOCUS ON
THIS ONE THING: FORGETTING THE PAST
AND LOOKING FORWARD TO WHAT LIES
AHEAD, I PRESS ON TO REACH THE END OF
THE RACE AND RECEIVE THE HEAVENLY PRIZE
FOR WHICH GOD, THROUGH CHRIST JESUS,
IS CALLING US.   *Philippians 3:13-14*

Grief

MY QUESTION *for* GOD

How can I help those who are grieving?

A MOMENT *with* GOD

Singing cheerful songs to a person with a heavy heart
is like taking someone's coat in cold weather or
pouring vinegar in a wound.   PROVERBS 25:20

*G*ive your attention, sympathy, and comfort to people who are grieving. Pretending that the pain is not there only adds insult to injury. It is difficult to be with someone who is grieving, but you don't need to come up with the "right" words to make it all go away—you can't. Your concern and your presence will help a grieving person more than words.

A cheerful heart is good medicine, but a broken spirit saps a person's strength.   PROVERBS 17:22

*B*e aware of the toll that grief takes on a person's spirit, mind, and body. Awareness leads to sympathy; sympathy leads to soothing the wounded; soothing leads to healing.

Be happy with those who are happy, and weep with those who weep.   ROMANS 12:15

*B*e sensitive to others' feelings. You can feel their sorrow as surely as you can feel their joy. But being too cheerful when others are grieving will only make them feel worse.

He comforts us in all our troubles so that we can comfort others. When they are troubled, we will be able to give them the same comfort God has given us.
                                              2 CORINTHIANS 1:4

*S*hare your own experiences of how God has comforted you. In doing so you may help others begin the healing process.

I have written and sent this short letter to you with the help of Silas, whom I commend to you as a faithful brother. My purpose in writing is to encourage you and assure you that what you are experiencing is truly part of God's grace for you.   1 PETER 5:12

*E*ncourage the brokenhearted. Words of comfort can lift up a hurting person.

How can your empty clichés comfort me? All your explanations are lies!   JOB 21:34

I have heard all this before. What miserable comforters you are!   JOB 16:2

*B*e careful with the words you say to those who are grieving. Explanations and clichés are rarely comforting. Love, sympathy, and the power of your presence are often more effective. Sometimes the best comfort you can give is just to be there.

DIVINE PROMISE

I WILL BE GLAD AND REJOICE IN YOUR UNFAILING LOVE, FOR YOU HAVE SEEN MY TROUBLES, AND YOU CARE ABOUT THE ANGUISH OF MY SOUL.   *Psalm 31:7*

Guarding Your Heart

MY QUESTION for GOD

What does it mean to guard my heart, and why is it important?

A MOMENT with GOD

Guard your heart above all else, for it determines the course of your life.
                                    PROVERBS 4:23

I say, anyone who even looks at a woman with lust has already committed adultery with her in his heart.
                                    MATTHEW 5:28

[Jesus] added, "It is what comes from inside that defiles you. For from within, out of a person's heart, come evil thoughts, sexual immorality . . . lustful desires."
                                    MARK 7:20-22

Your eye is a lamp that provides light for your body. When your eye is good, your whole body is filled with light.
                                    LUKE 11:34

*Y*our actions tell you the condition of your heart because that is where they begin. Left unchecked, wrong thoughts will eventually result in wrong actions. For example, if you allow yourself to think about having sex with someone who is not your spouse, your heart will begin to convince you that what you want to do is okay. The Bible says that the heart is "desperately wicked" (Jeremiah 17:9). In other words, don't trust

your heart to tell you what is right and good. Trust
God's Word; it comes from God's heart, which is good
and perfect.

DIVINE PROMISE

PRAY ABOUT EVERYTHING. TELL GOD WHAT
YOU NEED, AND THANK HIM FOR ALL HE HAS
DONE. THEN YOU WILL EXPERIENCE GOD'S
PEACE, WHICH EXCEEDS ANYTHING WE
CAN UNDERSTAND. HIS PEACE WILL GUARD
YOUR HEARTS AND MINDS AS YOU LIVE IN
CHRIST JESUS.   *Philippians 4:6-7*

Guilt

MY QUESTION *for* GOD

How can guilt be helpful?

A MOMENT *with* GOD

When you become aware of your guilt in any of these
ways, you must confess your sin.   LEVITICUS 5:5

Cleanse me from these hidden faults. Keep your
servant from deliberate sins! Don't let them control
me. Then I will be free of guilt.   PSALM 19:12-13

Only acknowledge your guilt. Admit that you
rebelled against the LORD your God.   JEREMIAH 3:13

A guilty conscience is a warning signal God has given you to tell you when you've done something wrong. Guilt leads you to confess your sins, indicating your desire to make things right and be forgiven. If you have no desire to have your sins forgiven, God will not forgive them. God often uses the feeling of guilt to tell you when you need to apologize. Leaders must not lose this important sense of guilt; otherwise they may not know when they have hurt or offended someone they work with. It is frustrating when people have a leader who is no longer self-aware and does not realize how their words and actions hurt others. If you are feeling guilty about something you have said or done that may have hurt someone, then now is the time to apologize and seek forgiveness. Act quickly so you do not become too desensitized to appropriate feelings of guilt. Ask God to reveal those actions and thoughts that displease him, even those you aren't aware of. When you confess where you were wrong, God removes your guilt, restores your joy, and heals broken relationships with those you have wronged.

DIVINE PROMISE

IF WE CONFESS OUR SINS TO HIM, HE IS
FAITHFUL AND JUST TO FORGIVE US OUR SINS
AND TO CLEANSE US FROM ALL WICKEDNESS.

1 John 1:9

Hand of God

MY QUESTIONS *for* GOD

Is God really at work all around me? How can I learn to see his hand in my life?

A MOMENT *with* GOD

Moses and Aaron did just as the LORD had commanded them. When Aaron raised his hand and struck the ground with his staff, gnats infested the entire land, covering the Egyptians and their animals. All the dust in the land of Egypt turned into gnats. Pharaoh's magicians tried to do the same thing with their secret arts, but this time they failed. And the gnats covered everyone, people and animals alike. "This is the finger of God!" the magicians exclaimed to Pharaoh. But Pharaoh's heart remained hard. He wouldn't listen to them, just as the LORD had predicted.   EXODUS 8:17-19

You won't see the hand of God in your life if you don't believe that miracles can happen today or that God will perform one on your behalf. Even Pharaoh's magicians saw the miraculous plague as an act of God, but Pharaoh was too stubborn to admit it. He convinced himself that there was some other explanation and that it couldn't be the hand of God. If you keep trying to explain away God's miracles, you won't see him at work. Instead of assuming that God couldn't possibly be interested in your work and life, start assuming that the little "miracles" around you are the work of his hand. Then you will be surprised to see how much God is doing in your life that you never noticed before.

DIVINE PROMISE

SEEK HIS WILL IN ALL YOU DO, AND HE WILL SHOW YOU WHICH PATH TO TAKE. *Proverbs 3:6*

Hard-Heartedness

MY QUESTION *for* GOD

What are the signs of a hard heart?

A MOMENT *with* GOD

Pharaoh's heart, however, remained hard. He still refused to listen, just as the LORD had predicted.

EXODUS 7:13

The older brother was angry and wouldn't go in. His father came out and begged him, but he replied, "All these years I've slaved for you and never once refused to do a single thing you told me to. And in all that time you never gave me even one young goat for a feast with my friends. Yet when this son of yours comes back after squandering your money on prostitutes, you celebrate by killing the fattened calf!" His father said to him, "Look, dear son, you have always stayed by me, and everything I have is yours. We had to celebrate this happy day. For your brother was dead and has come back to life! He was lost, but now he is found!"

LUKE 15:28-32

"Oh no, sir!" [Hannah] replied. "I haven't been drinking wine or anything stronger. But I am very discouraged, and I was pouring out my heart to the LORD."

1 SAMUEL 1:15

*P*haraoh had a hard, stubborn heart. No matter how much he heard about God or how many miracles he saw, he refused to believe. The older brother of the prodigal son also struggled with a hard heart; he was more eager to punish than forgive. Hannah, however, continued to pray to God even when it seemed God was not answering. As you evaluate the condition of your heart, you must ask yourself, is it becoming more hard and stubborn? Or is it open and pliable, reaching out to God no matter what your circumstances are? If you find it hard to forgive others or if you struggle to see God in your daily life, then your heart may be hardening. If you let it continue, you cut yourself off from God, your only lifeline and the only One who can really give you purpose and direction. A hard heart rejects the one thing that can save it—God's love. A tender heart seeks God's help and notices his perfectly timed responses.

DIVINE PROMISE

I WILL GIVE YOU A NEW HEART, AND I WILL PUT A NEW SPIRIT IN YOU. I WILL TAKE OUT YOUR STONY, STUBBORN HEART AND GIVE YOU A TENDER, RESPONSIVE HEART. *Ezekiel 36:26*

Holiness

MY QUESTION *for* GOD

Why is holiness important in the life of a leader?

A MOMENT *with* GOD

I am writing to God's church in Corinth, to you who
have been called by God to be his own holy people.
He made you holy by means of Christ Jesus, just as he
did for all people everywhere who call on the name of
our Lord Jesus Christ, their Lord and ours.

1 CORINTHIANS 1:2

You were cleansed; you were made holy; you were
made right with God by calling on the name of the
Lord Jesus Christ and by the Spirit of our God.

1 CORINTHIANS 6:11

I plead with you to give your bodies to God because
of all he has done for you. Let them be a living and
holy sacrifice—the kind he will find acceptable.

ROMANS 12:1

Now you must be holy in everything you do, just as
God who chose you is holy.   1 PETER 1:15

Make them holy by your truth; teach them your
word, which is truth.   JOHN 17:17

Think of holiness as both a journey and a final destination. To be completely holy is to be sinless, pure, and
perfect before God. Of course, no one can be perfect,

but that is our ultimate goal, and it will be our final
destination when we stand before God in heaven. Holiness also means to be different, to be set apart by God
for a specific purpose. It is much more than the absence of sin; it is the practice of righteousness, purity,
and godliness. Holiness means being wholly dedicated
and devoted to following God in a way that is distinct
and separate from the world's way of living. It is being
committed to right living and purity. You are to be
different from the rest of the world, and your life is a
journey toward becoming more pure and sinless, bit by
bit, with each passing day. As you make progress, you
also inspire those you lead to strive toward holiness.
When you strive to be holy during your earthly journey, you will one day arrive at your final destination to
stand holy before God.

DIVINE PROMISE

EVEN BEFORE HE MADE THE WORLD, GOD
LOVED US AND CHOSE US IN CHRIST TO BE
HOLY AND WITHOUT FAULT IN HIS EYES.
Ephesians 1:4

Humiliation

MY QUESTION *for* GOD

When I've been humiliated, how can I recover?

A MOMENT *with* GOD

The Philistines captured [Samson] and gouged out his eyes. They took him to Gaza, where he was bound with bronze chains and forced to grind grain in the prison.

JUDGES 16:21

Peter said, "Man, I don't know what you are talking about." And immediately, while he was still speaking, the rooster crowed. At that moment the Lord turned and looked at Peter. Then Peter remembered that the Lord had said, "Before the rooster crows tomorrow morning, you will deny three times that you even know me."

LUKE 22:60-62

I recognize my rebellion; it haunts me day and night.

PSALM 51:3

Oh, that my actions would consistently reflect your decrees! Then I will not be ashamed when I compare my life with your commands. . . . I cling to your laws. LORD, don't let me be put to shame! . . . Help me abandon my shameful ways; for your regulations are good. . . . May I be blameless in keeping your decrees; then I will never be ashamed.

PSALM 119:5-6, 31, 39, 80

Sometimes your own actions cause your humiliation, and sometimes you are humiliated by others. When you bring humiliation upon yourself, it goes deeper than just embarrassment. Embarrassment occurs when you do something, usually by accident, that is out of character and makes you feel self-conscious and distressed about what you did. On the other hand, humiliation occurs when you do something that utterly destroys your self-respect and dignity. For example, if you get caught stealing, you are humiliated in front of your family and friends, and you feel shame for what you did. Humiliation often brings guilt or shame because it reveals where sin has degraded your integrity. When others try to humiliate you, their objective is the same—to bring you shame or destroy your reputation. You can usually recover quickly from embarrassment, but it often takes much longer to recover from humiliation. If your enemies succeed in humiliating you, they can render you useless for a long time. No one likes to be humiliated, but it can be a divine moment for spiritual repentance and restoration because it forces you to go to the only One who can offer complete forgiveness and recovery. God promises to make you as clean as newly fallen snow and turn your humiliation into an opportunity for him to love, restore, and raise you up again. If you have experienced humiliation, especially if it was caused by your own sin, you may need to keep a low profile for a while to demonstrate that you are truly sorry and truly changed by the experience. But humiliation doesn't have to render you ineffective for God forever. He can and will restore you to integrity and service if you allow him.

DIVINE PROMISE

PRIDE ENDS IN HUMILIATION, WHILE
HUMILITY BRINGS HONOR. *Proverbs 29:23*

Humility

MY QUESTION *for* GOD

How can humility be helpful?

A MOMENT *with* GOD

Jacob prayed, ". . . I am not worthy of all the unfailing love and faithfulness you have shown to me, your servant. When I left home and crossed the Jordan River, I owned nothing except a walking stick. Now my household fills two large camps!"

GENESIS 32:9-10

Often when we prosper and all is well, we fall into pride and begin to think that we have achieved it all. Pride elevates you above others, even above God himself. But Jacob realized that he was not worthy of what he had. This is a mark of humility. Humility comes when you recognize that you need God and then acknowledge that God met your needs! God takes care of the humble. Humility is the honest recognition of your worth as God sees you, not as you wish to be seen by others. When you come to God in humility, your prayers will be answered. You are taking the important step of recognizing that God's will for your life will lead you toward what is good and right and away from sin and harm. You become humble when you realize your vulnerability before God and your complete dependence upon him.

THOSE WHO EXALT THEMSELVES WILL
BE HUMBLED, AND THOSE WHO HUMBLE
THEMSELVES WILL BE EXALTED.   *Matthew 23:12*

Hurt

MY QUESTION *for* GOD

How do I respond to those who hurt me?

A MOMENT *with* GOD

From that time on, Esau hated Jacob because their
father had given Jacob the blessing. And Esau began to
scheme: "I will soon be mourning my father's death.
Then I will kill my brother, Jacob." . . . Then Jacob
looked up and saw Esau coming with his 400 men.
. . . Then Jacob went on ahead. As he approached his
brother, he bowed to the ground seven times before
him. Then Esau ran to meet him and embraced him,
threw his arms around his neck, and kissed him. And
they both wept. . . . "My brother, I have plenty," Esau
answered. "Keep what you have for yourself."

GENESIS 27:41; 33:1-4, 9

*T*his reunion after years of separation could have been
the moment Esau was waiting for and Jacob was fear-
ing. Would Esau seek revenge over the pain Jacob had
caused him by stealing his birthright and blessing? Had
Esau held on to the resentment over the years? It is

refreshing to see Esau's change of heart when the two brothers finally meet again. Esau is content with what he has instead of being bitter over what he lost. Sometimes we feel that if we can forget the hurt, then we can forgive the person who hurt us. But forgiveness is not really about forgetting, which is often impossible. Instead, it is about surrendering your desire to hurt the other person as they hurt you. Forgiveness allows you to overcome the desire for retribution and releases you from anger, hurt, and bitterness. Leaders often falter when they can't let go of the hurt someone has caused them. It is only through forgiveness that you can deal with the hurt and move on.

DIVINE CHALLENGE

MAKE ALLOWANCE FOR EACH OTHER'S FAULTS,
AND FORGIVE ANYONE WHO OFFENDS YOU.
REMEMBER, THE LORD FORGAVE YOU, SO YOU
MUST FORGIVE OTHERS.   *Colossians 3:13*

Hypocrisy

MY QUESTION *for* GOD

How does hypocrisy hurt a leader?

A MOMENT *with* GOD

Samuel said, "What is this you have done?" Saul replied, "I saw my men scattering from me, and you didn't arrive when you said you would, and the

Philistines are at Micmash ready for battle. So I said,
'The Philistines are ready to march against us at
Gilgal, and I haven't even asked for the LORD's help!'
So I felt compelled to offer the burnt offering myself
before you came." "How foolish!" Samuel exclaimed.
"You have not kept the command the LORD your
God gave you. Had you kept it, the LORD would have
established your kingdom over Israel forever. But now
your kingdom must end, for the LORD has sought out
a man after his own heart."   1 SAMUEL 13:11-14

<hr />

To a thirsty, weary traveler, a mirage in the desert
sands gives the appearance of a pool of water—cool,
pure, life-giving. A closer look, however, reveals nothing
but dry ground. God hates hypocrisy because it is like
that mirage. What you see is not what you get. Hypocrisy gives the appearance of purity and integrity on the
outside when the heart is actually spiritually dry and
deceptive. Hypocrisy is pretending to be someone you
are not. Spiritual hypocrisy is pretending to be a godly
person when you really have selfish motives. You try to
look pious to others in order to gain something—a certain reputation, a business connection, or a position of
influence in the church or community. Hypocrisy is a
form of lying and deception, and it is fueled by pride
and selfishness. What God wants instead is sincerity and
honesty, which are fueled by humility. Hypocrisy can
cost a leader everything. It takes away the trust and credibility that are required to motivate others to follow you.
Divine moments can't come from hypocritical leaders.
God rejected Saul as king because of his hypocrisy. He

claimed to value God, but he was simply watching out for himself. Wise leaders are genuine leaders.

DIVINE CHALLENGE

WE CAN BE SURE THAT WE KNOW HIM IF WE OBEY HIS COMMANDMENTS. IF SOMEONE CLAIMS, "I KNOW GOD," BUT DOESN'T OBEY GOD'S COMMANDMENTS, THAT PERSON IS A LIAR AND IS NOT LIVING IN THE TRUTH. BUT THOSE WHO OBEY GOD'S WORD TRULY SHOW HOW COMPLETELY THEY LOVE HIM.   *1 John 2:3-5*

Imagination

MY QUESTION *for* GOD

How can I use my imagination to become a better leader?

A MOMENT *with* GOD

"Listen to me, all who hope for deliverance—all who seek the LORD! Consider the rock from which you were cut, the quarry from which you were mined. Yes, think about Abraham, your ancestor, and Sarah, who gave birth to your nation. Abraham was only one man when I called him. But when I blessed him, he became a great nation." The LORD will comfort Israel again and have pity on her ruins. Her desert will blossom like Eden, her barren wilderness like the garden of the LORD. Joy and gladness will be found there. Songs of thanksgiving will fill the air.

ISAIAH 51:1-3

*T*wo disciplines that help you grow stronger in your faith are remembering the past and looking forward to the future with a "holy imagination." God reminded his discouraged people that although Abraham and Sarah were old and infertile, God gave them a child, and from them came a great nation. Faith grows when you remember God's great acts recorded in Scripture and throughout the ages (see Hebrews 11), and when you trust that God will continue to perform great acts for his people today and in the future. Cultivating a holy imagination means letting God's promised hope of new and eternal life come alive in your mind, creating a vision of what God wants you to do. In the verses above, God promises to turn the deserts into lush land like the Garden of Eden. Not only will the barren places become fertile, but the curse of sin will be gone. God wanted the people to imagine what this new land would look like to give them a goal to work toward and a renewed vision and passion to get there. When you imagine a picture of what God is calling you to do, you will have a clearer goal of where he wants you to go and how to get there. If you can imagine what the final product will look like or what you want your team to accomplish, you will develop a better vision of what God wants to do through you. Imagination is necessary for vision. Ultimately, God wants you to imagine a life without the curse of sin and have faith that you will reach that life. Then your relationship with him will grow stronger.

DIVINE PROMISE

THAT IS WHAT THE SCRIPTURES MEAN
WHEN THEY SAY, "NO EYE HAS SEEN, NO EAR
HAS HEARD, AND NO MIND HAS IMAGINED
WHAT GOD HAS PREPARED FOR THOSE WHO
LOVE HIM."   *1 Corinthians 2:9*

Impossibilities

MY QUESTION *for* GOD

How do I deal with impossible situations?

A MOMENT *with* GOD

"Don't worry about this Philistine," David told
Saul. "I'll go fight him!" "Don't be ridiculous!" Saul
replied. "There's no way you can fight this Philistine
and possibly win! You're only a boy, and he's been a
man of war since his youth." . . . So David triumphed
over the Philistine with only a sling and a stone.

1 SAMUEL 17:32-33, 50

"The king's demand is impossible. No one except
the gods can tell you your dream, and they do not
live here among people." . . . Daniel replied, "There
are no wise men, enchanters, magicians, or fortune-
tellers who can reveal the king's secret. But there is a
God in heaven who reveals secrets, and he has shown
King Nebuchadnezzar what will happen in the future.
Now I will tell you your dream and the visions you
saw as you lay on your bed."   DANIEL 2:11, 27-28

Jesus soon saw a huge crowd of people coming to look for him. Turning to Philip, he asked, "Where can we buy bread to feed all these people?" He was testing Philip, for he already knew what he was going to do. Philip replied, "Even if we worked for months, we wouldn't have enough money to feed them!" Then Andrew, Simon Peter's brother, spoke up. "There's a young boy here with five barley loaves and two fish. But what good is that with this huge crowd?" "Tell everyone to sit down," Jesus said. So they all sat down on the grassy slopes. (The men alone numbered 5,000.) Then Jesus took the loaves, gave thanks to God, and distributed them to the people. Afterward he did the same with the fish. And they all ate as much as they wanted.   JOHN 6:5-11

In each of these situations, God's people had to deal with impossible problems. But in each case, the response involved open communication with God by acknowledging the impossible and obedience to God's response, whether it meant waiting or moving forward. God often uses what he has already given someone—a slingshot, a special ability, a loaf of bread—to accomplish the impossible. There is no doubt that God specializes in doing what from a human perspective seems impossible. But the limits of your abilities mark the beginning of his. The God who spoke all creation into existence can work miracles for you. You must believe that he can and that he wants to. Only God can do the impossible, but he often allows you to be involved in the process. Be open and ready to be used to accomplish whatever God has in mind!

DIVINE PROMISE

ALL GLORY TO GOD, WHO IS ABLE, THROUGH HIS MIGHTY POWER AT WORK WITHIN US, TO ACCOMPLISH INFINITELY MORE THAN WE MIGHT ASK OR THINK. *Ephesians 3:20*

Influence

MY QUESTION *for* GOD

How do my choices influence others?

A MOMENT *with* GOD

You yourself must be an example to them by doing good works of every kind. Let everything you do reflect the integrity and seriousness of your teaching.

TITUS 2:7

Let your good deeds shine out for all to see, so that everyone will praise your heavenly Father.

MATTHEW 5:16

Even more blessed are all who hear the word of God and put it into practice.

LUKE 11:28

*Y*our values influence your choices, and your choices influence your behavior. Your behavior reveals your heart, or what is most important to you. When you claim to be a follower of God, make sure that others can see that you are truly following him. Then many others will want to follow God as well because they like what they see in you. Ask a few of your closest friends or coworkers what kind of influence you have had lately on those around you.

DIVINE CHALLENGE

LET US THINK OF WAYS TO MOTIVATE
ONE ANOTHER TO ACTS OF LOVE AND
GOOD WORKS. *Hebrews 10:24*

Injustice

MY QUESTIONS *for* GOD

Why does a loving, sovereign God allow injustice? What can I do about injustice?

A MOMENT *with* GOD

You have wearied the LORD with your words. "How have we wearied him?" you ask. You have wearied him by saying that all who do evil are good in the LORD's sight, and he is pleased with them. You have wearied him by asking, "Where is the God of justice?"

MALACHI 2:17

How long, O LORD, must I call for help? But you
do not listen! "Violence is everywhere!" I cry, but
you do not come to save. . . . But you are pure and
cannot stand the sight of evil. Will you wink at their
treachery? Should you be silent while the wicked
swallow up people more righteous than they?

HABAKKUK 1:2, 13

If they twist justice in the courts—doesn't the LORD
see all these things?   LAMENTATIONS 3:36

Acquitting the guilty and condemning the
innocent—both are detestable to the LORD.

PROVERBS 17:15

Fear the LORD and judge with integrity, for the
LORD our God does not tolerate perverted justice,
partiality, or the taking of bribes.   2 CHRONICLES 19:7

*In*justice happens because God created human beings with free will. We have the freedom to choose
good or evil, right or wrong. If God hadn't done it that
way, we would only be puppets of a divine dictator, not
people who grow to love him. God knew that people
needed to have the freedom to choose. He also knew
that many would choose wrongly, causing injustice to
the innocent. But to think that God condones injustice
simply because it happens is contrary to his righteous
nature and opposed to what the Bible teaches about
sin. God sees every injustice, and he judges it as sin.
Leaders have a special responsibility to not look the
other way when they see injustice among those they

lead. They must do their part to fight injustice. When they do, they create divine moments not only in the lives of those they rescue but in the hearts of those who see it.

DIVINE PROMISE

THOSE WHO PLANT INJUSTICE WILL HARVEST DISASTER, AND THEIR REIGN OF TERROR WILL COME TO AN END.   *Proverbs 22:8*

Inspiration

MY QUESTION *for* GOD

How can I inspire the people I lead?

A MOMENT *with* GOD

Perhaps you will think to yourselves, "How can we ever conquer these nations that are so much more powerful than we are?" But don't be afraid of them! Just remember what the LORD your God did to Pharaoh and to all the land of Egypt.

DEUTERONOMY 7:17-18

If you obey, you will enjoy a long life in the land the LORD swore to give to your ancestors and to you, their descendants—a land flowing with milk and honey!   DEUTERONOMY 11:9

*Y*ou can inspire others by reminding them of God's past blessings, by presenting them with a positive vision of the future, and by speaking and acting in ways that show your complete confidence in the Lord's hand upon you and those you lead. By remembering how God has helped you in the past, you can help others get excited about the blessings awaiting them in the future. This sounds like simple advice, but often profound inspiration is achieved through the most basic measures.

DIVINE CHALLENGE

REMEMBER YOUR LEADERS WHO TAUGHT YOU
THE WORD OF GOD. THINK OF ALL THE GOOD
THAT HAS COME FROM THEIR LIVES, AND
FOLLOW THE EXAMPLE OF THEIR FAITH.
Hebrews 13:7

Integrity

MY QUESTION *for* GOD

How do I develop integrity in my life?

A MOMENT *with* GOD

This is a trustworthy saying: "If someone aspires to be an elder, he desires an honorable position." So an elder must be a man whose life is above reproach. He must be faithful to his wife. He must exercise self-control, live wisely, and have a good reputation. He must enjoy having guests in his home, and he must

be able to teach. He must not be a heavy drinker or
be violent. He must be gentle, not quarrelsome, and
not love money. He must manage his own family
well, having children who respect and obey him. . . .
Also, people outside the church must speak well of
him so that he will not be disgraced and fall into the
devil's trap.   1 TIMOTHY 3:1-4, 7

*P*aul lists numerous characteristics that are key to a life
of integrity, whether for church leaders or any Christian
in a leadership position. The common thread is consis-
tency between what people believe and how they live.
This is what is meant by integrity—the integration of
faith and life. Leaders should apply the truth of God's
Word to every aspect of their lives, especially in the
four primary areas we see in the passage above: Leaders should be mature in *personal spirituality,* exhibiting a
vibrant faith in Jesus Christ and ministering out of the
overflow of a deep knowledge of God; *emotional maturity,*
exercising self-control and effectively managing anger,
conflict, ambition, finances, and excesses (such as alcohol); *relational responsibility,* valuing people and relationships, especially within their families, and being gracious
hosts; and *ministry competency,* being knowledgeable and
skilled in communicating God's truth and love to others.
These high standards do not mean that spiritual leaders
must be perfect but that they must be committed to integrity in all aspects of life.

DIVINE PROMISE

THE LORD REWARDED ME FOR DOING RIGHT.
HE HAS SEEN MY INNOCENCE. TO THE
FAITHFUL YOU SHOW YOURSELF FAITHFUL;
TO THOSE WITH INTEGRITY YOU SHOW
INTEGRITY.   *Psalm 18:24-25*

Investing

MY QUESTION *for* GOD

What should I invest in?

A MOMENT *with* GOD

[Jesus] told them a story: "A rich man had a fertile
farm that produced fine crops. He said to himself,
'What should I do? I don't have room for all my
crops.' Then he said, 'I know! I'll tear down my
barns and build bigger ones. Then I'll have room
enough to store all my wheat and other goods. And
I'll sit back and say to myself, "My friend, you have
enough stored away for years to come. Now take it
easy! Eat, drink, and be merry!"' But God said to
him, 'You fool! You will die this very night. Then
who will get everything you worked for?' Yes, a
person is a fool to store up earthly wealth but not
have a rich relationship with God."   LUKE 12:16-21

How dangerous it is to be a success in the world
but a failure with God! Leaders constantly fight this

temptation because they are pushed even more than others to be successful in this life. But to gain the world and lose your soul is the ultimate failure, for your soul is eternal but all the things of this world will pass away. It takes a truly wise investor to learn what kind of investing needs to be done now in order to gain wealth and success in eternity. Spend as much time studying how to invest in your spiritual life into eternity as you spend thinking about your earthly investments in your savings or retirement accounts. You can't afford to risk losing everything because you invested in the wrong things.

DIVINE PROMISE

IF YOU TRY TO HANG ON TO YOUR LIFE, YOU WILL LOSE IT. BUT IF YOU GIVE UP YOUR LIFE FOR MY SAKE, YOU WILL SAVE IT. AND WHAT DO YOU BENEFIT IF YOU GAIN THE WHOLE WORLD BUT LOSE YOUR OWN SOUL? IS ANYTHING WORTH MORE THAN YOUR SOUL?   *Matthew 16:25-26*

MY QUESTIONS *for* GOD

If God promises me joy, does that mean I'll always be happy? What if I don't feel happy?

A MOMENT *with* GOD

Always be full of joy in the Lord. I say it again—rejoice! . . . I know how to live on almost nothing or

with everything. I have learned the secret of living in
every situation, whether it is with a full stomach or
empty, with plenty or little.   PHILIPPIANS 4:4, 12

When troubles come your way, consider it an
opportunity for great joy.   JAMES 1:2

𝒢od does not promise constant happiness. In fact, the
Bible assures us that problems will come because of the
fallen world in which we live. But God does promise
lasting joy for all who faithfully follow him. This kind of
joy is possible despite your problems because you know
that God is with you to help you through them and that
someday he will take them all away. You can have lasting
joy even when you have temporary unhappiness. This is
what it means to live with an eternal perspective. Leaders who discover this secret to joy never let problems
get the best of them because they can see that a problem
is just another opportunity to learn, grow stronger, and
ultimately be more successful. This also inspires those
they lead to find ways to overcome problems rather
than be discouraged by them. Joy can change everyone's
perspective on problems that interfere with happiness.
When that happens, it can truly be a divine moment!

DIVINE PROMISE

THOSE WHO LOOK TO HIM FOR HELP WILL BE
RADIANT WITH JOY; NO SHADOW OF SHAME
WILL DARKEN THEIR FACES. . . . TASTE AND SEE
THAT THE LORD IS GOOD. OH, THE JOYS OF
THOSE WHO TAKE REFUGE IN HIM!   *Psalm 34:5, 8*

Judging Others

What's the difference between judging others and offering constructive criticism?

A MOMENT *with* GOD

Do not judge others, and you will not be judged. For you will be treated as you treat others. The standard you use in judging is the standard by which you will be judged. And why worry about a speck in your friend's eye when you have a log in your own?

MATTHEW 7:1-3

Don't speak evil against each other, dear brothers and sisters. If you criticize and judge each other, then you are criticizing and judging God's law. But your job is to obey the law, not to judge whether it applies to you.

JAMES 4:11

*O*ne coach berates a player publicly for making a mistake in a game. Another coach waits until the game is over and privately tells the player how to avoid making the same mistake again. Though no one likes criticism—even when it is constructive—we sometimes need it. It is much easier to receive criticism when it is offered gently and in love rather than in a harsh or humiliating way. To judge others is to criticize with no intent of seeing them succeed or improve. To offer constructive criticism is to have the goal of building a relationship and helping that person become who God created him or her to be. Constructive criticism can bring a divine moment of change. Judging others is hurtful, and it helps no one.

DIVINE PROMISE

MAKE ALLOWANCE FOR EACH OTHER'S FAULTS, AND FORGIVE ANYONE WHO OFFENDS YOU. REMEMBER, THE LORD FORGAVE YOU, SO YOU MUST FORGIVE OTHERS.   *Colossians 3:13*

Knowledge

MY QUESTION *for* GOD

How can I use my knowledge most effectively?

A MOMENT *with* GOD

Fear of the LORD is the foundation of true knowledge, but fools despise wisdom and discipline.

PROVERBS 1:7

Cry out for insight, and ask for understanding. Search for them. . . . Then you will understand what it means to fear the LORD, and you will gain knowledge of God.

PROVERBS 2:3-5

We live in a culture driven by the pursuit of information. Finding information is easy, but what you do with that knowledge is what counts. Simply having knowledge isn't helpful if you don't use it for something good. This principle applies especially to leaders who want to go beyond just doing their jobs and want to make an impact for God. You might know a lot about the Bible. You might know the difference between right and wrong. You might even know Bible history and theology. But if you don't apply this knowledge toward making a positive difference in your life and the lives of others, it goes to waste. The book of Proverbs in the Bible declares that the fear of the Lord is the beginning of knowledge, meaning that your understanding of information and of the world should first pass through the filter of God's Word. Since God is omniscient—he has *all* knowledge—you can respect the accuracy and authority of his Word. You fear the Lord when you respect what he says. Only then will you develop the godly application of your knowledge.

DIVINE PROMISE

[JESUS SAID,] "ANYONE WHO LISTENS TO
MY TEACHING AND FOLLOWS IT IS WISE,
LIKE A PERSON WHO BUILDS A HOUSE ON
SOLID ROCK. THOUGH THE RAIN COMES
IN TORRENTS AND THE FLOODWATERS RISE
AND THE WINDS BEAT AGAINST THAT HOUSE,
IT WON'T COLLAPSE BECAUSE IT IS BUILT
ON BEDROCK." *Matthew 7:24-25*

Leadership

MY QUESTION for GOD

What are some qualities of a good leader?

A MOMENT with GOD

The LORD had said to Abram, "Leave your native country, your relatives, and your father's family, and go to the land that I will show you." . . . So Abram departed as the LORD had instructed.   GENESIS 12:1, 4

A good leader follows the Lord's leading.

Choose today whom you will serve. . . . As for me and my family, we will serve the LORD.   JOSHUA 24:15

A good leader demonstrates God's character by example.

How can I deal with all your problems and bickering? Choose some well-respected men from each tribe who are known for their wisdom and understanding, and I will appoint them as your leaders.

DEUTERONOMY 1:12-13

A good leader delegates responsibilities to trustworthy subordinates.

I pressed further, "What you are doing is not right!"

NEHEMIAH 5:9

A good leader courageously confronts those who are doing wrong.

Jesus told them, "In this world the kings and great men lord it over their people, yet they are called 'friends of the people.' But among you it will be different. Those who are the greatest among you should take the lowest rank, and the leader should be like a servant."   LUKE 22:25-26

A good leader leads by serving, not by giving orders.

It was only right that he should make Jesus, through his suffering, a perfect leader, fit to bring them into their salvation.   HEBREWS 2:10

A good leader is even more effective after enduring and overcoming hard times.

Then David said to God, "I have sinned greatly by taking this census."   1 CHRONICLES 21:8

*G*ood leaders accept responsibility for their actions.

He prayed three times a day, just as he had always done.   DANIEL 6:10

*G*ood leaders maintain good habits.

He did what was pleasing in the LORD's sight and followed the example of his ancestor David. He did not turn away from doing what was right.   2 KINGS 22:2

A good leader consistently does the right thing.

He must become greater and greater, and I must become less and less.   JOHN 3:30

*G*ood leaders do not emphasize themselves.

Listen, you leaders of Israel! You are supposed to know right from wrong.   MICAH 3:1

*G*ood leaders are know the difference between right and wrong.

Let us go on instead and become mature in our understanding.   HEBREWS 6:1

*G*ood leaders demonstrate maturity and wisdom.

The following men joined David. . . . They were among the warriors who fought beside David in battle. All of them were expert archers.

1 CHRONICLES 12:1-2

*G*ood leaders are not threatened by skilled subordinates. They purposely gather skillful people around them.

Dear brothers and sisters, not many of you should become teachers in the church, for we who teach will be judged more strictly.   – JAMES 3:1

Good leaders hold themselves to a higher standard of accountability.

Fools think their own way is right, but the wise listen to others.   PROVERBS 12:15

Good leaders take good advice and act on it. They are more concerned about the right way than their own way.

If anyone comes to your meeting and does not teach the truth about Christ, don't . . . give any kind of encouragement.   2 JOHN 1:10

Good leaders recognize false teaching and boldly combat it.

Uphold the rights of the oppressed and the destitute.
                                                 PSALM 82:3

Good leaders support righteousness and justice.

I gave the responsibility of governing Jerusalem to my brother Hanani, . . . for he was a faithful man who feared God more than most.   NEHEMIAH 7:2

Good leaders show faithfulness and reverence.

Whoever wants to be a leader among you must be your servant.   MATTHEW 20:26

*G*ood leaders have a servant's heart.

King Hezekiah and the prophet Isaiah . . . cried out
in prayer to God in heaven.   2 Chronicles 32:20

*G*ood leaders rely on prayer.

No one can lay any foundation other than the one we
already have—Jesus Christ.   1 Corinthians 3:11

*G*ood leaders have their foundation in Jesus.

Be strong and courageous! . . . For the Lord your
God is with you wherever you go.   Joshua 1:9

*G*ood leaders are courageous because they have the
assurance of God's presence.

Divine Promise

I WILL GIVE YOU SHEPHERDS AFTER MY
OWN HEART, WHO WILL GUIDE YOU WITH
KNOWLEDGE AND UNDERSTANDING. *Jeremiah 3:15*

Letting Go

My Question *for* God

How can I learn to let go of my need to be in control?

A MOMENT *with* GOD

Everything is wearisome beyond description. No
matter how much we see, we are never satisfied.
No matter how much we hear, we are not content.

ECCLESIASTES 1:8

I gave up in despair, questioning the value of all my
hard work in this world.   ECCLESIASTES 2:20

*F*rustration comes when you limit God's work in
your life. If you feel the need to control every little
detail of your life and the end result of all your efforts,
reality will always fall short, especially in your own
eyes. Don't let your expectations for yourself exceed
what you can actually achieve. After you have done
your best, you must let go and trust God to complete
the work he has asked you to start. Letting go of your
control means accepting God's best for you, even when
things don't turn out as you hoped.

DIVINE PROMISE

BY HIS DIVINE POWER, GOD HAS GIVEN US
EVERYTHING WE NEED FOR LIVING A GODLY
LIFE. WE HAVE RECEIVED ALL OF THIS BY
COMING TO KNOW HIM, THE ONE WHO
CALLED US TO HIMSELF BY MEANS OF HIS
MARVELOUS GLORY AND EXCELLENCE.   *2 Peter 1:3*

Limitations

MY QUESTION *for* GOD

How can my limitations actually help me as a leader?

A MOMENT *with* GOD

Asa cried out to the LORD his God, "O LORD, no one but you can help the powerless against the mighty! Help us, O LORD our God, for we trust in you alone. It is in your name that we have come against this vast horde. O LORD, you are our God; do not let mere men prevail against you!"   2 CHRONICLES 14:11

O Lord, hear their threats, and give us, your servants, great boldness in preaching your word. Stretch out your hand with healing power; may miraculous signs and wonders be done through the name of your holy servant Jesus.   ACTS 4:29-30

Moses pleaded with the LORD, "O Lord, I'm not very good with words. I never have been, and I'm not now, even though you have spoken to me. I get tongue-tied, and my words get tangled." Then the LORD asked Moses, "Who makes a person's mouth? Who decides whether people speak or do not speak, hear or do not hear, see or do not see? Is it not I, the LORD? Now go! I will be with you as you speak, and I will instruct you in what to say."   EXODUS 4:10-12

As a kid, you may have dreamed of being able to fly or having X-ray vision, like Superman. As an adult, such fantasies remind you of your human limitations. The more you age, the more you begin to understand the limits of your body, as it becomes harder to do the things that once were easy—running, walking up the stairs, reading small print. You also begin to realize your emotional limitations. A traumatic event may paralyze you or knock you into a daze. Many times, difficult circumstances can drain you emotionally and cause depression, anxiety, or apathy. Throughout the Bible, when God's people and their leaders suddenly realized their limitations, they responded immediately with earnest prayer and then trusted God to act on their behalf. In God's unlimited knowledge, he created us with limitations, not to discourage us, but to help us realize our utter need for him. It is in weakness that God's strength shines. Then when you accomplish something great despite your limitations, it is obvious that God is working through you, and others are led to give him the credit. Jesus tells us, "What is impossible for people is possible with God" (Luke 18:27). The next time life throws your limitations in your face, don't become discouraged. Instead, see it as an opportunity for God's power to defy your limitations, and then enjoy the divine moment of having him work through you to accomplish more than you ever could have dreamed.

DIVINE PROMISE

EACH TIME [THE LORD] SAID, "MY GRACE IS ALL YOU NEED. MY POWER WORKS BEST IN WEAKNESS." SO NOW I AM GLAD TO BOAST ABOUT MY WEAKNESSES, SO THAT THE POWER OF CHRIST CAN WORK THROUGH ME.

2 Corinthians 12:9

Listening

MY QUESTION *for* GOD

Why is listening important?

A MOMENT *with* GOD

My child, listen when your father corrects you. Don't neglect your mother's instruction. What you learn from them will crown you with grace and be a chain of honor around your neck.　　　PROVERBS 1:8-9

Listening helps you grow and mature. Listening fosters learning, which leads to knowledge and wisdom.

Oh, why didn't I listen to my teachers? Why didn't I pay attention to my instructors?　　　PROVERBS 5:13

Listening helps keep you accountable. When you listen to good advice, you absorb it with your mind and your heart. It will come in handy at just the right time, when you are most vulnerable to temptation.

My child, listen to what I say. . . You will find the
right way to go.   PROVERBS 2:1, 9

*L*istening to God is essential for making good decisions. When you truly listen to the Holy Spirit and to
God's commands, you will have the guidance you need
to make wise choices.

Listen to me! For I have important things to tell you.
                                          PROVERBS 8:6

*L*istening keeps you from being closeminded. It gives
you the opportunity to hear a variety of ideas from different sources. The more you listen, the better your chances
of hearing a nugget of wisdom. God's truth is found in
God's Word, but the application of it is often found by
listening to the advice and experiences of others.

Moses listened to his father-in-law's advice and
followed his suggestions.   EXODUS 18:24

Everyone listened to my advice.   JOB 29:21

*L*istening shows that you respect others. It honors
someone as a person. People feel affirmed when they've
been heard.

Those who shut their ears to the cries of the poor will
be ignored in their own time of need.   PROVERBS 21:13

*L*istening is more than hearing. Listening connects you with others. It helps you understand their needs and find the best way to help them.

DIVINE PROMISE

COME AND LISTEN TO MY COUNSEL. I'LL SHARE MY HEART WITH YOU AND MAKE YOU WISE.
Proverbs 1:23

Loneliness

MY QUESTION *for* GOD

Now that I've made it to the top, why does it feel so lonely?

A MOMENT *with* GOD

Turn to me and have mercy, for I am alone and in deep distress.   PSALM 25:16

I can't carry all these people by myself! The load is far too heavy!   NUMBERS 11:14

I am the only one left.   1 KINGS 19:14

Couldn't you watch with me even one hour?

MATTHEW 26:40

*I*t can be lonely at the top partially because the leader is often the only one who understands the all the struggles of the organization, the cares of the people, and the demands of the big picture. The leader feels ultimately responsible for the future of the group and the success of the project. Leaders may also feel lonely because they're not sure who they can trust. The people you depend on sometimes desert you, abandon you, or turn away from you. Often there may be only a few people you can truly count on, and sometimes there may not be any. Another part of the loneliness of being a leader comes from the hesitation to get too close to those you lead. You may believe that friendships could inhibit your ability to lead. The reverse is also true. The people you lead may not want to get too close to you because of your position of authority over them. Leadership can often be all-consuming, and that is another cause of the loneliness. To deal with the loneliness at the top, it is essential for you to have a life outside of your work, where you can develop friendships and a support network. Be vulnerable with those you lead. Most people assume that the leader has it all together, but the reality is that you, too, are a person seeking to be faithful to God in a fallen world. Sharing your weaknesses and struggles will usually rally your people to come alongside you and help you accomplish what you can't do on your own. If you see vulnerability as a negative thing, you will likely have trouble relating to others. But if you view it as a way to develop deeper and healthier relationships, you will decrease your loneliness.

DIVINE PROMISE

EVEN WHEN I WALK THROUGH THE DARKEST VALLEY . . . YOU ARE CLOSE BESIDE ME.

Psalm 23:4

Meditation

MY QUESTION *for* GOD

Why is it important for pastors to spend time studying and meditating on God's Word?

A MOMENT *with* GOD

On October 8 Ezra the priest brought the Book of the Law before the assembly, which included the men and women and all the children old enough to understand. He faced the square just inside the Water Gate from early morning until noon and read aloud to everyone who could understand. All the people listened closely to the Book of the Law. Ezra the scribe stood on a high wooden platform that had been made for the occasion . . . then instructed the people in the Law while everyone remained in their places . . . and clearly explained the meaning of what was being read, helping the people understand each passage.   NEHEMIAH 8:2-4, 7-8

With the wall of Jerusalem finished, the people wanted to continue to enjoy God's blessing and not fall into sin again. So they assembled, hungry to hear God's

Word. Whom did they ask to read the Word? Ezra, who was a scribe—someone who had devoted his life to studying the Scriptures. The people could count on Ezra to explain God's Word clearly and accurately. The Bible is still the authoritative guide for how to know God and live God's way. Like the Israelites, we need individuals who are experts in the Bible and can share their knowledge with us. Sometimes church members complain about how much time pastors spend studying. However, many churches should give their pastors even more time to increase their knowledge of the Bible. If pastors are going to feed their flocks, they must have time to feed themselves. For biblical knowledge and spiritual insights to come out of a pastor's mouth, they must first be in his mind and heart. We must make sure our spiritual leaders have more than budgets and administrative tasks on their minds. They need the very wisdom of God, and that comes from Bible study and meditation on the very words of God.

DIVINE PROMISE

YOU HAVE BEEN TAUGHT THE HOLY SCRIPTURES FROM CHILDHOOD, AND THEY HAVE GIVEN YOU THE WISDOM TO RECEIVE THE SALVATION THAT COMES BY TRUSTING IN CHRIST JESUS. ALL SCRIPTURE IS INSPIRED BY GOD AND IS USEFUL TO TEACH US WHAT IS TRUE AND TO MAKE US REALIZE WHAT IS WRONG IN OUR LIVES. IT CORRECTS US WHEN WE ARE WRONG AND TEACHES US TO DO WHAT IS RIGHT. GOD USES IT TO PREPARE AND EQUIP HIS PEOPLE TO DO EVERY GOOD WORK. *2 Timothy 3:15-17*

Mentoring

MY QUESTION *for* GOD

How is a leader also a mentor?

A MOMENT *with* GOD

Moses and his assistant Joshua set out, and Moses climbed up the mountain of God.   EXODUS 24:13

Inside the Tent of Meeting, the LORD would speak to Moses face to face, as one speaks to a friend. Afterward Moses would return to the camp, but the young man who assisted him, Joshua son of Nun, would remain behind in the Tent of Meeting.   EXODUS 33:11

You have heard me teach things that have been confirmed by many reliable witnesses. Now teach these truths to other trustworthy people who will be able to pass them on to others.   2 TIMOTHY 2:2

[Jesus said,] "When the Father sends the Advocate as my representative—that is, the Holy Spirit—he will teach you everything and will remind you of everything I have told you."   JOHN 14:26

A mentoring relationship has the specific formula of one person teaching and another person learning. Good mentors commit to building a relationship with someone who is younger or has less life experience. Through this relationship, a mentor shares wisdom, life experiences, and support with the goal of helping the mentee learn and grow. Moses and Joshua are an example of an effective mentoring relationship. First, Moses oversaw Joshua's active involvement in the work God gave them. Second, Moses welcomed Joshua into his own spiritual arena, even allowing Joshua to be with him during his most significant experiences with God. This created divine moments of spiritual growth. Then, when Moses died, it was clear that Joshua was prepared to assume responsibility as a faithful, fully equipped, credible leader. Leaders don't live forever, but the work of the Lord must continue from generation to generation. Mentoring ensures that continuation of God's work. The Holy Spirit is our ultimate spiritual mentor. It is through the Holy Spirit that Jesus helps us build a relationship with God and guides us into wisdom, maturity, and understanding.

DIVINE PROMISE

FOOLS THINK THEIR OWN WAY IS RIGHT, BUT THE WISE LISTEN TO OTHERS.   *Proverbs 12:15*

Mercy

MY QUESTION *for* GOD

Mercy seems like such an outdated concept. How does it affect my daily life?

A MOMENT *with* GOD

The LORD is compassionate and merciful, slow to get angry and filled with unfailing love.   PSALM 103:8

Sin is no longer your master, for you no longer live under the requirements of the law. Instead, you live under the freedom of God's grace.   Romans 6:14

Let us come boldly to the throne of our gracious God. There we will receive his mercy, and we will find grace to help us when we need it most.

Hebrews 4:16

*M*ercy is another word for the amazing kindness God showers on us, even when we do not deserve it. God's greatest act of kindness is to offer us salvation and eternal life, even though at times we have ignored him, neglected him, and rebelled against him. When God forgives you, his mercy sets you free from the power of sin so that you can choose each day to over-power your sinful nature. God's mercy changes your life when you understand what it feels like to be loved even when you have not loved in return. When you understand the mercy God has shown you, it will cause you to love others in the same way, creating in their lives a divine moment. Determine to be an example of God's mercy to someone else today.

Divine Promise
I PROMISE THIS VERY DAY THAT I WILL REPAY TWO BLESSINGS FOR EACH OF YOUR TROUBLES.
Zechariah 9:12

Mistakes

MY QUESTION *for* GOD

What should leaders do when they make mistakes?

A MOMENT *with* GOD

David summoned the priests, Zadok and Abiathar, and these Levite leaders: Uriel, Asaiah, Joel, Shemaiah, Eliel, and Amminadab. He said to them, "You are the leaders of the Levite families. You must purify yourselves and all your fellow Levites, so you can bring the Ark of the LORD, the God of Israel, to the place I have prepared for it. Because you Levites did not carry the Ark the first time, the anger of the LORD our God burst out against us. We failed to ask God how to move it properly."   1 CHRONICLES 15:11-13

In this passage, David admitted that he had not prayed to God to ask for direction the first time he tried to bring the Ark to Jerusalem (see chapter 13). Even though he had conferred with the leaders of Israel, he had not asked God how and when they should move the Ark. This mistake resulted in a fatal tragedy with the death of Uzzah. David is a good example to any leader who has made an error. A leader's honest and frank admission of his or her mistakes is the only way to recover from errors in judgment. It helps the entire community to learn from the mistake, and it inspires people to admit their own mistakes to each other as well.

DIVINE PROMISE

FINALLY, I CONFESSED ALL MY SINS TO YOU
AND STOPPED TRYING TO HIDE MY GUILT.
I SAID TO MYSELF, "I WILL CONFESS MY
REBELLION TO THE LORD." AND YOU FORGAVE
ME! ALL MY GUILT IS GONE.   *Psalm 32:5*

Morale

MY QUESTION *for* GOD

What can I do to boost morale?

A MOMENT *with* GOD

The whole community began weeping aloud, and
they cried all night. Their voices rose in a great
chorus of protest against Moses and Aaron. "If
only we had died in Egypt, or even here in the
wilderness!" they complained. "Why is the LORD
taking us to this country only to have us die in battle?
Our wives and our little ones will be carried off as
plunder! Wouldn't it be better for us to return to
Egypt?" Then they plotted among themselves, "Let's
choose a new leader and go back to Egypt!" . . .
Two of the men who had explored the land, Joshua
son of Nun and Caleb . . . said to all the people of
Israel, "The land we traveled through and explored
is a wonderful land! And if the LORD is pleased with
us, he will bring us safely into that land and give it to
us. It is a rich land flowing with milk and honey. Do
not rebel against the LORD, and don't be afraid of the

people of the land. They are only helpless prey to us!
They have no protection, but the LORD is with us!
Don't be afraid of them!"   NUMBERS 14:1-9

*P*eople need encouragement when they stand at life's
crossroads, when they feel that life's challenges are
stronger than they are. The Israelites stood at the edge
of the Promised Land—should they enter it despite the
challenges, or should they turn back? Despite God's
promise to give them victory, the discouragers far out-
numbered the encouragers. Morale took a nosedive.
It's easy to become discouraged when you stop looking
at everything God has given you and focus instead on
the obstacles before you. Low morale breeds discouragement, and discouragement can cause everyone to
doubt God's love, drawing them away from the source
of greatest help. Like Caleb, you can encourage others
and boost morale by reminding them what God can do
and wants to do for and through them. Encouragement
inspires people to do their best and to be gracious, loving, and encouraging to others.

DIVINE PROMISE

A CHEERFUL LOOK BRINGS JOY TO THE HEART;
GOOD NEWS MAKES FOR GOOD HEALTH.

Proverbs 15:30

Motives

MY QUESTION for GOD

Does God care about my motives as long as I do the right thing?

A MOMENT with GOD

I know, my God, that you examine our hearts and rejoice when you find integrity there. You know I have done all this with good motives.   1 CHRONICLES 29:17

The sacrifice of an evil person is detestable, especially when it is offered with wrong motives.   PROVERBS 21:27

When you give to someone in need, don't let your left hand know what your right hand is doing. Give your gifts in private, and your Father, who sees everything, will reward you.   MATTHEW 6:3-4

Think of some reasons why someone might donate a large sum of money to a charity. One person might do it in order to earn a tax break; another might do it to win political favor; still another might do it out of deep compassion for the poor. The same act can be set in motion by very different motives. God is as interested in your motives as he is in your behavior, because selfish and sinful motives eventually produce selfish and sinful behavior. Leaders might be tempted to find an excuse for doing almost anything for the cause, but God looks behind the excuses to the motives of the heart. Check your motives before you act. Ask yourself, would God be pleased with my real reasons for doing this? Would I still be willing to do this if I knew everyone would find out? Your motives definitely make a difference in your ability to lead well and gain the respect of those you lead.

DIVINE PROMISE

THE LORD'S LIGHT PENETRATES THE HUMAN SPIRIT, EXPOSING EVERY HIDDEN MOTIVE.
Proverbs 20:27

Negotiation

MY QUESTION *for* GOD

What are some godly principles for negotiation?

A MOMENT *with* GOD

Do not defraud or rob your neighbor. Do not make your hired workers wait until the next day to receive their pay.   LEVITICUS 19:13

Do to others whatever you would like them to do to you.   MATTHEW 7:12

The LORD demands accurate scales and balances; he sets the standards for fairness.   PROVERBS 16:11

Boaz went to the town gate and took a seat there. . . . "Come over here and sit down, friend. I want to talk to you." . . . Then Boaz called ten leaders from the town and asked them to sit as witnesses. . . . Then

Boaz said to the elders and to the crowd standing
around, "You are witnesses that today I have bought
from Naomi all the property of Elimelech, Kilion,
and Mahlon."   RUTH 4:1-2, 9

*Treat others as you would want them to treat you,
with honesty and fairness in all your dealings. You
should not ask, "Am I getting everything I can get out
of this deal?" Instead ask, "Is this deal fair for all parties?" This attitude may not be well accepted in many
businesses today, but the alternative is to compromise
your integrity. The personal cost to you is great when
you do that. Almost anything is easier to restore than
damaged integrity. Knowing that you have maintained
your integrity throughout a negotiation is a divine moment when you feel the God's approval. You can be
sure that you have pleased your real boss.*

DIVINE PROMISE

PEOPLE WITH INTEGRITY WALK SAFELY, BUT
THOSE WHO FOLLOW CROOKED PATHS WILL
SLIP AND FALL.   *Proverbs 10:9*

Obedience

MY QUESTION *for* GOD

*Total obedience to God is impossible. How obedient do I need
to be in order to please him?*

A MOMENT *with* GOD

Obey me, and I will be your God, and you will be my
people. Do everything as I say, and all will be well!

JEREMIAH 7:23

Moses said, "This is what the LORD has commanded
you to do so that the glory of the LORD may appear
to you."

LEVITICUS 9:6

If you look carefully into the perfect law that sets you
free, and if you do what it says and don't forget what
you heard, then God will bless you for doing it.

JAMES 1:25

God knows you can't obey him completely, so he is
more interested in how much you *want* to obey him.
To want to obey him more, you must grasp a true
understanding of obedience and how it builds or destroys relationships. From the six-year-old who leaves
her playmates because her mother has called her in for
dinner to the business executive who pays his taxes on
time, we all live in a web of relationships that depend
upon obedience to authority. Like a loving parent or
a responsible government, God sets standards of behavior for your own good and to protect you from evil
and harm. Some people defy authority, but obedience
actually frees us to enjoy life as God intended because
it keeps us from becoming entangled in harmful situations. Even though God's commandments are sometimes difficult to obey, or they don't make sense from
our human perspective, obedience to him will always

bring blessing, joy, and peace. When you look at obedience this way, then you obey God out of love and gratitude for all he's trying to do for you rather than out of fear of being punished. The more you obey out of love, the more you want to obey, and the more that obedience becomes a lifestyle rather than a chore. The more that obedience becomes a lifestyle, the less you are tempted to avoid the consequences of poor decisions. Since God is the creator of life, he knows how life is supposed to work. Obedience to his ways demonstrates your willingness to follow through on what he says is best. It shows your trust that God's way will work for you, and that will inspire the people you lead.

DIVINE PROMISE

OH, THE JOYS OF THOSE WHO DO NOT FOLLOW
THE ADVICE OF THE WICKED, OR STAND
AROUND WITH SINNERS, OR JOIN IN WITH
MOCKERS. BUT THEY DELIGHT IN THE LAW OF
THE LORD, MEDITATING ON IT DAY AND NIGHT.
THEY ARE LIKE TREES PLANTED ALONG THE
RIVERBANK, BEARING FRUIT EACH SEASON.
THEIR LEAVES NEVER WITHER, AND THEY
PROSPER IN ALL THEY DO. *Psalm 1:1-3*

Opportunities

MY QUESTION *for* GOD

How can I make the most of the opportunities that come my way?

A MOMENT *with* GOD

Make the most of every opportunity in these
evil days.   EPHESIANS 5:16

A hard worker has plenty of food, but a person who
chases fantasies has no sense.   PROVERBS 12:11

In the meantime, I will be staying here at Ephesus
until the Festival of Pentecost. There is a wide-
open door for a great work here, although many
oppose me.   1 CORINTHIANS 16:8-9

In many ways, life is defined by opportunities seized
or missed. According to the Bible, we are to take advantage of opportunities by responding with bold action when we recognize them as God-given chances
to participate in his purpose. We should always be
prepared to recognize and act upon the opportunities
God offers us to be used by and for him. When you
believe that God is presenting you with an opportunity,
respond quickly and work hard to maximize the situation he has put before you. Be willing to rearrange your
agenda in order to take advantage of any God-given
opportunity. Think of how God might use you because
you've made yourself available for his work. Keep your
eyes open for what God will bring your way.

DIVINE PROMISE
WE MUST QUICKLY CARRY OUT THE TASKS
ASSIGNED US BY THE ONE WHO SENT US.
THE NIGHT IS COMING, AND THEN NO ONE
CAN WORK. *John 9:4*

Organization

MY QUESTION *for* GOD

Wouldn't the church be better off without boards and committees and formal organization?

A MOMENT *with* GOD

The leaders of the people were living in Jerusalem, the holy city. A tenth of the people from the other towns of Judah and Benjamin were chosen by sacred lots to live there, too, while the rest stayed where they were. And the people commended everyone who volunteered to resettle in Jerusalem. Here is a list of the names of the provincial officials who came to live in Jerusalem.   NEHEMIAH 11:1-3

I left you on the island of Crete so you could complete our work there and appoint elders in each town as I instructed you.   TITUS 1:5

As the believers rapidly multiplied, there were rumblings of discontent. The Greek-speaking believers complained about the Hebrew-speaking believers, saying that their widows were being discriminated against in the daily distribution of food. So the Twelve called a meeting of all the believers. They said, "We apostles should spend our time teaching the word of God, not running a food program. And so, brothers, select seven men who are well respected and are full of the Spirit and wisdom. We will give them this responsibility. Then we apostles can spend our time in prayer and teaching the word."   ACTS 6:1-4

$\mathscr{I}$n the Nehemiah passage above, the exiled Jews wanted to be a unified and effective people of God, not just a mob of random refugees. This involved careful organization. Every organization needs some kind of structure to be effective. This has been true of the church from its earliest days. Sometimes church boards or committees become ponderous or paralyzing. When this happens, it may be necessary to restructure creatively. But churches need some form of organization if they are going to mobilize Christians to advance Christ's kingdom and experience a breakthrough in God's work among them. Getting things done requires effective organization.

DIVINE PROMISE

WHEN YOU MEET TOGETHER, ONE WILL SING, ONE WILL TEACH, ANOTHER WILL TELL SOME SPECIAL REVELATION GOD HAS GIVEN, ONE WILL SPEAK IN TONGUES, AND ANOTHER WILL INTERPRET WHAT IS SAID. BUT EVERYTHING THAT IS DONE MUST STRENGTHEN ALL OF YOU. . . . FOR GOD IS NOT A GOD OF DISORDER BUT OF PEACE, AS IN ALL THE MEETINGS OF GOD'S HOLY PEOPLE.

1 Corinthians 14:26, 33

Overwhelmed

MY QUESTION *for* GOD

What should I do when I feel overwhelmed?

A MOMENT *with* GOD

Five of you will chase a hundred, and a hundred of you will chase ten thousand! All your enemies will fall beneath your sword.   LEVITICUS 26:8

Each one of you will put to flight a thousand of the enemy, for the LORD your God fights for you, just as he has promised.   JOSHUA 23:10

When you feel overwhelmed, remember that the power of God is on your side, regardless of the number of enemies against you. Knowing that God works through your weaknesses and limitations can be a great encouragement. No matter how weak or insignificant you may feel, God can do great things through you.

We also pray that you will be strengthened with all his glorious power so you will have all the endurance and patience you need. May you be filled with joy, always thanking the Father. He has enabled you to share in the inheritance that belongs to his people, who live in the light. For he has rescued us from the kingdom of darkness and transferred us into the Kingdom of his dear Son.   COLOSSIANS 1:11-13

When you feel overwhelmed, remember that you have been rescued from sin's control and Satan's power. God, through the power of his Holy Spirit, has given you all you need to overcome whatever overwhelms you. When you remember that you are already free from sin's power, the problems of this world lose their power over you.

DIVINE PROMISE

GOD IS OUR REFUGE AND STRENGTH, ALWAYS READY TO HELP IN TIMES OF TROUBLE. *Psalm 46:1*

Past

MY QUESTION *for* GOD

I can't seem to shake some things from my past. Can God help me overcome them?

A MOMENT *with* GOD

When I refused to confess my sin, my body wasted away, and I groaned all day long. Day and night your hand of discipline was heavy on me. My strength evaporated like water in the summer heat. Finally, I confessed all my sins to you and stopped trying to hide my guilt. I said to myself, "I will confess my rebellion to the LORD." And you forgave me! All my guilt is gone.   PSALM 32:3-5

I will delight in your decrees and not forget your
word. . . . I will never forget your commandments,
for by them you give me life.   PSALM 119:16, 93

Though your sins are like scarlet, I will make them
as white as snow. Though they are red like crimson,
I will make them as white as wool.   ISAIAH 1:18

The past is like a photo album containing snapshots of every moment of your life. These snapshots
show not just your happy moments and celebrations,
but also your failures, tragedies, and acts of deepest
shame. Most of us would like to lock away some parts
of our past or tear out the snapshots that expose the
moments we'd like to forget. The apostle Paul, who
is one of the greatest leaders in the New Testament,
had a past he wished he could forget. His album was
full of snapshots recording his days of persecuting and
killing Christians. Paul could have been burdened with
immense regret, but he understood that his past had
been redeemed through God's healing and forgiveness.
How you view your past will affect how you live in the
present and in the future. It even affects how you lead.
Some of us have a past containing a strong spiritual
heritage from loving parents and mentors. Don't take
that for granted; use it to help and minister to others.
Some of us have a past filled with regrets over actions
that were wrong or hurtful. No matter what you've
done, God is ready to forgive you, cleanse you of sin
and guilt, and give you a new start—fully forgiven.
Your difficult life journey, along with your experience

of God's unconditional forgiveness, can help you be an even more effective leader. God wants to throw away all the bad snapshots and give you a new present and future—and he can if you'll let him. God can remove your regret, guilt, and shame, and you can be free to live in peace with purpose and joy.

DIVINE PROMISE

I WILL FORGIVE THEIR WICKEDNESS, AND I
WILL NEVER AGAIN REMEMBER THEIR SINS.
Hebrews 8:12

Patience

MY QUESTION *for* GOD

How can I be more patient?

A MOMENT *with* GOD

May God, who gives this patience and encouragement, help you live in complete harmony with each other, as is fitting for followers of Christ Jesus.   ROMANS 15:5

Be patient with each other, making allowance for each other's faults because of your love.   EPHESIANS 4:2

We also pray that you will be strengthened with all his glorious power so you will have all the endurance and patience you need.   COLOSSIANS 1:11

*P*atience and perspective go hand in hand. When you are always focused on your own agenda and priorities, you will often find yourself impatient because life will rarely go the way you want it to. This is especially true for leaders, who are constantly dealing with unexpected events and interruptions. When you take the broader perspective that life is a winding journey and not a straight line between two points, you realize that what you do along the way is often as important as getting to your destination. This gives you patience when things aren't going the way you'd like and helps you welcome opportunities to serve others on the detours of daily life. What you see as life's detours may be God's chosen path for you.

DIVINE CHALLENGE

REJOICE IN OUR CONFIDENT HOPE. BE PATIENT IN TROUBLE, AND KEEP ON PRAYING.   *Romans 12:12*

Peace

MY QUESTION *for* GOD

How can I make peace with others?

A MOMENT *with* GOD

God blesses those who work for peace.   MATTHEW 5:9

Work for . . . peace and prosperity.   JEREMIAH 29:7

When you go through deep waters, I will be
with you.   ISAIAH 43:2

*P*eace is not the absence of conflict; it is the confident assurance in the middle of conflict. Peace comes from dealing with conflict appropriately. God calls us to pursue peace, which sometimes involves hard work. God then blesses us when we bring his peace to others.

Be joyful. Grow to maturity. Encourage each other. Live in harmony and peace. Then the God of love and peace will be with you.   2 CORINTHIANS 13:11

*W*ork hard at getting rid of sin in your own life and diligently building others up to help achieve peace.

Make every effort to keep yourselves united in the Spirit, binding yourselves together with peace.

EPHESIANS 4:3

*W*ork toward the kind of unity with others that comes only from the Holy Spirit.

The wisdom from above is . . . peace loving, gentle at all times, and willing to yield to others. It is full of mercy and good deeds. It shows no favoritism and is always sincere.   JAMES 3:17

*C*ommit yourself to the gentle deeds that are the mark of a true peacemaker.

Look at those who are honest and good, for a wonderful future awaits those who love peace.

PSALM 37:37

Never pay back evil with more evil. . . . Do all that you can to live in peace with everyone.   ROMANS 12:17-18

*I*f you harbor feelings of revenge in your heart, you cannot be at peace with others. Bitterness and revenge can never bring peace.

Deceit fills hearts that are plotting evil; joy fills hearts that are planning peace!   PROVERBS 12:20

*P*roactively pursuing peace is one of the surest ways to release streams of joy into your heart.

DIVINE PROMISE

I AM LEAVING YOU WITH A GIFT—PEACE OF MIND AND HEART.   *John 14:27*

Perfection

MY QUESTION *for* GOD

Even though I try so hard, I know I am less than perfect. Can God still use me?

A MOMENT *with* GOD

After looking in all directions to make sure no one was watching, Moses killed the Egyptian and hid the body in the sand.   EXODUS 2:12

Jonah got up and went in the opposite direction to get away from the LORD.   JONAH 1:3

Peter swore, "A curse on me if I'm lying—I don't know the man!"   MATTHEW 26:74

So, my dear brothers and sisters, be strong and immovable. Always work enthusiastically for the Lord, for you know that nothing you do for the Lord is ever useless.   1 CORINTHIANS 15:58

If you keep yourself pure, you will be a special utensil for honorable use. Your life will be clean, and you will be ready for the Master to use you for every good work.   2 TIMOTHY 2:21

Carefully determine what pleases the Lord.

EPHESIANS 5:10

*P*erfection is not a requirement for God to use you. He can use anyone and any circumstance he chooses to bring about his will. In the verses above, we read about the failures of Moses, Jonah, and Peter. Yet God used each of them in a mighty way to carry out his work and plans. God knew the future sins of these men before he chose them to become his leaders. But he also knew that they longed to have a clean heart and right relationship with him, even though they stumbled in their faith. Fortunately, God can accomplish holy work through unholy people, because he knows no one is perfect. He will use you if you sincerely want to be close to him and be used by him, even though he knows your inadequacies and future failures. The key to being used by God is not perfection but a willingness to repent of sin, seek forgiveness, and serve with humility and obedience. Then worry and frustration diminish and purpose and fulfillment increase.

DIVINE PROMISE

I DON'T MEAN TO SAY THAT I HAVE ALREADY ACHIEVED THESE THINGS OR THAT I HAVE ALREADY REACHED PERFECTION. BUT I PRESS ON TO POSSESS THAT PERFECTION FOR WHICH CHRIST JESUS FIRST POSSESSED ME.   *Philippians 3:12*

Perseverance

MY QUESTION *for* GOD

Why is perseverance important?

A MOMENT *with* GOD

Let's not get tired of doing what is good. At just the right time we will reap a harvest of blessing if we don't give up.   GALATIANS 6:9

Those who remain in me, and I in them, will produce much fruit.   JOHN 15:5

Perseverance leads to a productive life. Giving up leads to the frustration of unfinished work. When you persevere, you can look back with satisfaction on a full and fruitful life.

It would be good for you to finish what you started a year ago. Last year you were the first who wanted to give, and you were the first to begin doing it. Now you should finish what you started. Let the eagerness you showed in the beginning be matched now by your giving.   2 CORINTHIANS 8:10-11

*P*erseverance validates your promises and demonstrates your credibility.

Keep on asking, and you will receive what you ask for. Keep on seeking, and you will find. Keep on knocking, and the door will be opened to you.   MATTHEW 7:7

*G*od honors perseverance in prayer. All perseverance is wrapped in expectant hope for the future. Perseverance in prayer demonstrates your faith that God is listening, that he cares, and that he will respond.

We can rejoice, too, when we run into problems and trials, for we know that they help us develop endurance. And endurance develops strength of character, and character strengthens our confident hope of salvation.   ROMANS 5:3-4

*P*erseverance helps you deal with adversity by making you stronger. Without adversity, there would be nothing to exercise the muscles of your faith. Ask God to give you a glimpse of what he wants you to learn as you persevere through difficult times.

Even when we are weighed down with troubles,
it is for your comfort and salvation! For when we
ourselves are comforted, we will certainly comfort
you. Then you can patiently endure the same things
we suffer.   2 CORINTHIANS 1:6

Stand firm against him, and be strong in your faith.
Remember that your Christian brothers and sisters
all over the world are going through the same kind of
suffering you are.   1 PETER 5:9

*P*erseverance encourages others to be patient, work
hard, and remain faithful. When they see the benefits
of a life of perseverance, they will want the same, now
and for eternity.

DIVINE PROMISE

DEAR BROTHERS AND SISTERS, NEVER GET
TIRED OF DOING GOOD.   *2 Thessalonians 3:13*

Perspective

MY QUESTIONS *for* GOD

*How do I make sense of the seemingly random circumstances
of my life? Is God really in charge, or do things happen
by chance?*

A Moment *with* God

I am Joseph, your brother, whom you sold into
slavery in Egypt. But don't be upset, and don't be
angry with yourselves for selling me to this place.
It was God who sent me here ahead of you to preserve
your lives. . . . So it was God who sent me here,
not you!   GENESIS 45:4-5, 8

The LORD will work out his plans for my life.

PSALM 138:8

From a human perspective, the world and even our
lives often seem to be random and unpredictable, but
God is ultimately in control. In Joseph's story, God
used even the cruel and unjust actions of Joseph's own
brothers to fulfill his plan. People's sinful ways do not
ruin God's sovereign plans. Your life is like a tapestry.
Now you can see only small sections on the back, with
all its knots and loose ends. Someday you will see the
front in its entirety, the beautiful picture of world history and your personal story from God's perspective.
If you can see unexpected and even unwelcome circumstances in this way, you can embrace both the good
and the bad, knowing that God is weaving a beautiful
picture with your life.

DIVINE PROMISE

YOU SEE ME WHEN I TRAVEL AND WHEN I REST
AT HOME. YOU KNOW EVERYTHING I DO.
Psalm 139:3

Planning

Should I spend my time praying instead of planning?

A MOMENT *with* GOD

The king . . . asked, "How long will you be gone?
When will you return?" After I told him how long I
would be gone, the king agreed to my request. I also
said to the king, "If it please the king, let me have
letters addressed to the governors of the province
west of the Euphrates River, instructing them to let
me travel safely through their territories on my way
to Judah. And please give me a letter addressed to
Asaph, the manager of the king's forest, instructing
him to give me timber. I will need it to make beams
for the gates of the Temple fortress, for the city walls,
and for a house for myself." And the king granted
these requests, because the gracious hand of God was
on me.   NEHEMIAH 2:6-8

Prayer is of paramount importance, but planning
is still necessary. When Nehemiah had the chance to
speak to the king, he was able to spell out how long his
mission would take, what documents he would need,
and even the method of construction he would use.
The specificity and intelligence of Nehemiah's replies
was undoubtedly a factor in the king's granting of his
requests. Prayer and planning are partners. As you pray
for God's help, ask God to show you how you should

proceed. Draw up a plan so that when God provides an opportunity, you will be ready to move forward.

DIVINE CHALLENGE

DON'T BEGIN UNTIL YOU COUNT THE COST.
FOR WHO WOULD BEGIN CONSTRUCTION OF
A BUILDING WITHOUT FIRST CALCULATING
THE COST TO SEE IF THERE IS ENOUGH MONEY
TO FINISH IT?   *Luke 14:28*

Potential

MY QUESTION *for* GOD

How does God help me reach the potential he sees in me?

A MOMENT *with* GOD

Gideon . . . was threshing wheat at the bottom of a winepress to hide the grain from the Midianites. The angel of the LORD appeared to him and said, "Mighty hero, the LORD is with you! . . . Go with the strength you have, and rescue Israel from the Midianites. I am sending you!" "But LORD," Gideon replied, "how can I rescue Israel? . . . I am the least in my entire family!"   JUDGES 6:11-12, 14-15

The angel of the Lord greeted Gideon by calling him a "mighty hero." Was God talking to the right person?

This was Gideon, who was hiding from his enemies, who saw himself as the least significant member of his family. But God knew the potential he had given Gideon, and he called him to use it. God calls out the best in you, and he sees more in you than you see in yourself. You may look at your limitations, but God looks at your potential. If you want to reach your full potential, learn to see yourself through God's eyes. He sees you for what he intended you to be.

DIVINE PROMISE

I CAN DO EVERYTHING THROUGH CHRIST, WHO GIVES ME STRENGTH.   *Philippians 4:13*

Power

MY QUESTION *for* GOD

When can power become dangerous?

A MOMENT *with* GOD

Let's build a great city for ourselves with a tower that reaches into the sky. This will make us famous and keep us from being scattered all over the world.

GENESIS 11:4

O Egypt, to which of the trees of Eden will you compare your strength and glory? You, too, will be brought down to the depths with all these other nations. You will lie there among the outcasts who have died by the sword. This will be the fate of Pharaoh and all his hordes. I, the Sovereign LORD, have spoken!   EZEKIEL 31:18

*P*ower is intoxicating—with it comes recognition, control, and often wealth. These feed pride, and pride leads you away from God and into sin. This is why power so often corrupts. If you are in a position of power or authority, two things will help you use it wisely: accountability and service. When you have to explain your motives to others, you will be more careful about what you do and say. When you determine to serve others with your power rather than be served, you will gain great support and loyalty from those you lead.

DIVINE PROMISE

IT IS NOT THAT WE THINK WE ARE QUALIFIED TO DO ANYTHING ON OUR OWN. OUR QUALIFICATION COMES FROM GOD.
2 Corinthians 3:5

Prayer

MY QUESTION *for* GOD

What role should prayer play in a leader's life?

A MOMENT *with* GOD

As for me, I will certainly not sin against the LORD
by ending my prayers for you. And I will continue to
teach you what is good and right.   1 SAMUEL 12:23

$\mathcal{L}$eaders should consistently pray for those they lead.

Moses tried to pacify the LORD his God. "O LORD!"
he said. "Why are you so angry with your own people
whom you brought from the land of Egypt with such
great power and such a strong hand?" . . . So the
LORD changed his mind about the terrible disaster he
had threatened.   EXODUS 32:11, 14

$\mathcal{L}$eaders should pray for the Lord's mercy upon their
people. This does not mean they shouldn't confront the
people's sin, however. Moses' intercession saved the dis-
obedient Israelites from the punishment of God's wrath.

Solomon stood before the altar of the LORD in front
of the entire community of Israel. He lifted his hands
toward heaven, and he prayed, "O LORD, God of
Israel, there is no God like you in all of heaven above
or on the earth below. You keep your covenant and
show unfailing love to all who walk before you in
wholehearted devotion."   1 KINGS 8:22-23

$\mathcal{L}$eaders should not be afraid to pray in public. It reminds their people that they can depend on the promises and power of God.

Jehoshaphat was terrified by this news and begged the LORD for guidance. He also ordered everyone in Judah to begin fasting. So people from all the towns of Judah came to Jerusalem to seek the LORD's help. Jehoshaphat stood before the community of Judah and Jerusalem in front of the new courtyard at the Temple of the LORD. He prayed, "O LORD, God of our ancestors, you alone are the God who is in heaven. You are ruler of all the kingdoms of the earth. You are powerful and mighty; no one can stand against you! . . . We are powerless against this mighty army that is about to attack us. We do not know what to do, but we are looking to you for help."   2 CHRONICLES 20:3-6, 12

*L*eaders should pray when they don't know exactly what to do or when they don't have the resources they need to handle a situation or a crisis.

[Jesus said,] "Simon, Simon, Satan has asked to sift each of you like wheat. But I have pleaded in prayer for you, Simon, that your faith should not fail. So when you have repented and turned to me again, strengthen your brothers."   LUKE 22:31-32

*L*eaders should pray for the spiritual strength and well-being of those they lead.

We have not stopped praying for you since we first heard about you. We ask God to give you complete knowledge of his will and to give you spiritual wisdom.   COLOSSIANS 1:9

*L*eaders should pray for the spiritual growth and maturity of those they lead.

DIVINE PROMISE

**THE LORD IS CLOSE TO ALL WHO CALL ON HIM,
YES, TO ALL WHO CALL ON HIM IN TRUTH.**
Psalm 145:18

Preparation

MY QUESTION *for* GOD

How does God prepare me to do what he calls me to do?

A MOMENT *with* GOD

May the God of peace—who brought up from the dead our Lord Jesus, the great Shepherd of the sheep, and ratified an eternal covenant with his blood—may he equip you with all you need for doing his will. May he produce in you, through the power of Jesus Christ, every good thing that is pleasing to him.

HEBREWS 13:20-21

All Scripture is inspired by God. . . . God uses it to prepare and equip his people to do every good work.

2 TIMOTHY 3:16-17

*I*t can be extremely frustrating to be given an assignment without the resources to accomplish it. But when God calls you to a task, he equips you for it. If you have

tuned yourself to hear his voice, you can be sure that he
will give you the resources to fulfill the work he calls you
to. He has given you counsel and direction in his Word,
special abilities and gifts to use as you pursue your assignment, and his Holy Spirit to give you strength and guidance along the way. But you must tap into the resources
he has given you. Then you will be fully prepared.

When her son was born, she named him Samson.
And the LORD blessed him as he grew up. And the
Spirit of the LORD began to stir him while he lived in
Mahaneh-dan, which is located between the towns
of Zorah and Eshtaol. . . . So the Philistines captured
him and gouged out his eyes. They took him to Gaza,
where he was bound with bronze chains and forced to
grind grain in the prison.   JUDGES 13:24-25; 16:21

Be strong in the Lord and in his mighty power. Put
on all of God's armor so that you will be able to stand
firm against all strategies of the devil.   EPHESIANS 6:10-11

Study this Book of Instruction continually. Meditate
on it day and night so you will be sure to obey
everything written in it. Only then will you prosper
and succeed.   JOSHUA 1:8

*A*s soon as Samson was born, God's Spirit began to
work in him to get his attention. God wanted to prepare
Samson for a unique job, and Samson was supposed to
do his part in return—listen for God's voice, obey his
clear instructions, and act upon the opportunities God
would bring to him. Sadly, Samson didn't do this, and

he never reached his full potential. What is the Spirit of the Lord preparing you for? The key to recognizing his work in your life is first to obey God's clear instructions for living, found in the Bible. If you obey God, your life will go in the right direction, and you will be prepared to walk through the doors of opportunity he opens for you.

DIVINE PROMISE

PUT ON THE PEACE THAT COMES FROM THE
GOOD NEWS SO THAT YOU WILL BE FULLY
PREPARED.   *Ephesians 6:15*

Presence of God

MY QUESTION *for* GOD

What are the benefits of being in God's presence?

A MOMENT *with* GOD

The LORD replied, "I will personally go with you, Moses, and I will give you rest—everything will be fine for you."   EXODUS 33:14

When Moses came down Mount Sinai carrying the two stone tablets inscribed with the terms of the covenant, he wasn't aware that his face had become radiant because he had spoken to the LORD.

EXODUS 34:29

Because of Christ and our faith in him, we can now come boldly and confidently into God's presence.

EPHESIANS 3:12

When you pray, I will listen. If you look for me wholeheartedly, you will find me.   JEREMIAH 29:12-13

*M*oses literally glowed from being in God's presence. He understood that without God's presence he was nothing more than a mere human. If he was going to be able to take God's people on a divine journey and follow God's call, he knew he had better follow God's lead. The only way to follow God is to stay within his presence, which means to keep your focus on him. Keeping your eyes on God ensures that you stay close to him, and it takes you in the direction he wants you to go. God's presence also refreshes you by giving you rest, peace and strength. It helps you align your thoughts with God's thoughts so you can know his will. Sometimes you may not want God quite that close because it might mean a radical change in your lifestyle. But if you could see the end result of living daily in God's presence, you wouldn't want to wait to get started!

DIVINE CHALLENGE
SING PRAISES TO GOD AND TO HIS NAME!
. . . HIS NAME IS THE LORD—REJOICE IN HIS
PRESENCE! *Psalm 68:4*

Pride

MY QUESTION *for* GOD

How can I tell if I am struggling with pride?

A MOMENT *with* GOD

Then Pharaoh summoned Moses and Aaron and begged, "Plead with the LORD to take the frogs away from me and my people. I will let your people go, so they can offer sacrifices to the LORD." . . . So Moses and Aaron left Pharaoh's palace, and Moses cried out to the LORD about the frogs he had inflicted on Pharaoh. And the LORD did just what Moses had predicted. The frogs in the houses, the courtyards, and the fields all died. The Egyptians piled them into great heaps, and a terrible stench filled the land. But when Pharaoh saw that relief had come, he became stubborn. He refused to listen to Moses and Aaron, just as the LORD had predicted.   EXODUS 8:8, 12-15

*W*ith each plague that God brought upon Egypt, Pharaoh's resolve weakened—temporarily. Pharaoh tried to negotiate a number of pleas to let Israel go without setting them free. He tried to maintain control over the situation because he refused to acknowledge the sovereign authority of Israel's God. Only the final plague of the death of the firstborn shook Pharaoh's illusion of power. We all have an area in our lives where we are a little like Pharaoh, where we want to be in charge and make our own rules. But just as there can be only one driver in a car, so there is room for only

one God in every heart. To discover pride in your life,
discern those areas where you are still making the rules
instead of living by God's rules, the areas where you
need to give up control to God. If you can do this, you
will save yourself much grief and avoid fighting against
God—a battle you cannot win.

DIVINE PROMISE

WHAT SORROW FOR THOSE WHO ARE WISE
IN THEIR OWN EYES AND THINK THEMSELVES
SO CLEVER.   *Isaiah 5:21*

Problems

MY QUESTION *for* GOD

How should I deal with problems among those I lead?

A MOMENT *with* GOD

I arrived in Jerusalem. Three days later, I slipped
out during the night, taking only a few others with
me. I had not told anyone about the plans God had
put in my heart for Jerusalem. We took no pack
animals with us except the donkey I was riding. After
dark I went out . . . to inspect the broken walls and
burned gates.   NEHEMIAH 2:11-13

Too often, leaders try to address a problem without
fully understanding it. It's no wonder, then, when they

have trouble enlisting people to help. This can be a pitfall
for new leaders in particular. As soon as Nehemiah arrived in Jerusalem, he took the time to gather firsthand
information about the state of the city wall he had returned to build. Likewise, leaders must do their home-
work, or they will become frustrated when their people
don't rally behind an unclear cause. For leaders to be
effective, information must precede mobilization.

While they were at Hazeroth, Miriam and Aaron
criticized Moses because he had married a Cushite
woman. They said, "Has the LORD spoken only
through Moses? Hasn't he spoken through us, too?"
But the LORD heard them. (Now Moses was very
humble—more humble than any other person
on earth.) So immediately the LORD called to
Moses, Aaron, and Miriam and said, "Go out to the
Tabernacle, all three of you!" So the three of them
went to the Tabernacle. Then the LORD descended
in the pillar of cloud and stood at the entrance of the
Tabernacle. "Aaron and Miriam!" he called, and they
stepped forward. And the LORD said to them, "Now
listen to what I say."   NUMBERS 12:1-6

𝒪ne drop of poison can taint an entire meal. One
tiny cancer cell, left unchecked, can grow into a life-
threatening disease. Unresolved problems are the same
way—they soon affect everything and everyone. They
affect your health, thoughts, and relationships. In the
passage above, God couldn't let this problem with authority fester, especially because it directly affected the

leaders of his people. He immediately intervened to deal directly with the issue. He focused on the real issue and then properly balanced discipline with mercy. As difficult as it is, you must deal with unresolved problems quickly before they consume you and the people you lead.

DIVINE CHALLENGE

SHARE EACH OTHER'S BURDENS, AND IN THIS WAY OBEY THE LAW OF CHRIST.   *Galatians 6:2*

Productivity

MY QUESTION *for* GOD

How can I be more productive?

A MOMENT *with* GOD

They delight in the law of the LORD. . . . They are like trees planted along the riverbank, bearing fruit each season. Their leaves never wither, and they prosper in all they do.   PSALM 1:2-3

A tree is identified by its fruit. . . . A good person produces good things from the treasury of a good heart.   LUKE 6:44-45

But the Holy Spirit produces this kind of fruit in our lives.   GALATIANS 5:22

A branch cannot produce fruit if it is severed from the vine, and you cannot be fruitful unless you remain in me.

JOHN 15:4

*P*roductivity is almost universally measured in numbers. How many widgets were produced? How many sold? How much profit was earned? We measure productivity, even in our personal lives, in quantitative, objective terms. How much have our houses gained in equity since we bought them? How many A's do our children receive on their report cards? How many items did we cross off our to-do lists today? This view of productivity is fine and good, and it helps us evaluate work performance and personal achievement. But the Bible defines productivity not only in terms of numbers but in terms of relationships and character. Just like an apple can look good on the outside but actually be full of worms, so a person's external appearance of goodness does not measure the authenticity of the heart. False pretenses of goodness or pretending to be spiritual actually shows a rotten core that cannot be productive. A godly heart is the key to true productivity, which means producing good deeds. When all is said and done, what you do for God is the only bottom line that really matters.

DIVINE PROMISE

TO THOSE WHO USE WELL WHAT THEY ARE GIVEN, EVEN MORE WILL BE GIVEN. *Matthew 25:29*

Purpose

MY QUESTION *for* GOD

Does God have a specific purpose for me?

A MOMENT *with* GOD

I cry out to God Most High, to God who will fulfill
his purpose for me.   PSALM 57:2

My life is worth nothing to me unless I use it for
finishing the work assigned me by the Lord Jesus.

ACTS 20:24

You didn't choose me. I chose you. I appointed you to
go and produce lasting fruit, so that the Father will
give you whatever you ask for, using my name.

JOHN 15:16

I take joy in doing your will, my God, for your
instructions are written on my heart.   PSALM 40:8

I press on to possess that perfection for which Christ
Jesus first possessed me.   PHILIPPIANS 3:12

*D*o you make to-do lists of the things that you need
to accomplish each day, week, or month? Such lists
can help bring a sense of purpose to your life, helping
you stay focused and on target. If you were to reduce
the most important tasks of your entire life to a list of
only three or four items, what would they be? The first
item on that list should come very close to identifying
the purpose of your life. According to the Bible, your

purpose should be inspired by a vision of how God can best use you to accomplish his goals. God has a general purpose and a specific purpose for you. In general, as a Christian you have been chosen by God to let the love of Jesus shine through you to make an impact on others. More specifically, God has given you certain spiritual gifts and wants you to use them to make a unique contribution within your sphere of influence. The more you fulfill your general purpose, the more clear your specific purpose will become. The ultimate goal in life is not to reach the destination you want but to reach the destination God wants for you. As you passionately pursue the purpose that God assigned you, he promises that your life will have lasting meaning, significance, and eternal results.

DIVINE PROMISE

LET GOD TRANSFORM YOU INTO A NEW PERSON BY CHANGING THE WAY YOU THINK. THEN YOU WILL LEARN TO KNOW GOD'S WILL FOR YOU, WHICH IS GOOD AND PLEASING AND PERFECT. *Romans 12:2*

Questions

MY QUESTION *for* GOD

What are some key questions I should ask myself each day?

A Moment *with* God

Search for the LORD and for his strength; continually seek him.   PSALM 105:4

Shouldn't people ask God for guidance?   ISAIAH 8:19

Hear me as I pray, O LORD. Be merciful and answer me!   PSALM 27:7

Are you the Messiah we've been expecting, or should we keep looking for someone else?   MATTHEW 11:3

The crowds asked, "What should we do?"   LUKE 3:10

*P*erhaps nothing reveals the heart of human emotion more than the questions we are asking every day. Questions reveal who we are, what we're thinking about, what we long to know, and what drives us. Do you ask God for wisdom and guidance? Do you question whether your work is self-serving or serving God? Have you asked God what he wants you to do with your time, energy, and resources? When you regularly ask God questions like these and have an open mind and heart, you will find the answers you need to live a life that pleases God.

DIVINE PROMISE

THIS IS WHAT THE LORD SAYS . . . : ASK ME AND I WILL TELL YOU REMARKABLE SECRETS YOU DO NOT KNOW ABOUT THINGS TO COME.
Jeremiah 33:2-3

Quiet

Why is it important to have quiet time?

A MOMENT *with* GOD

Be still, and know that I am God! I will be honored by every nation. I will be honored throughout the world.

PSALM 46:10

Finding times to be quiet and meditate will help you recognize the voice of God when he speaks.

Then Jesus said, "Let's go off by ourselves to a quiet place and rest awhile." He said this because there were so many people coming and going that Jesus and his apostles didn't even have time to eat. So they left by boat for a quiet place, where they could be alone.

MARK 6:31-32

Jesus saw the importance of rest and reflection. Life should have a balance of work and rest, of spending time with others and having quiet time for restoration.

Only in returning to me and resting in me will you be saved. In quietness and confidence is your strength.

ISAIAH 30:15

Quiet time is crucial to renewing your relationship with God and being restored by spending time with him. Connecting with God taps into his strength. Maybe you find it difficult to rest. You mistakenly believe that productivity requires constant activity. But sometimes you need to slow down in order to speed up. You need to stop for a while to let your body, mind, and spirit recover and reset your course so that you can be more energized and more productive when you get back to the work at hand.

When you pray, go away by yourself, shut the door behind you, and pray to your Father in private. Then your Father, who sees everything, will reward you.

MATTHEW 6:6

*Y*ou need quiet times to pray. Take a few moments to escape from the busy world so you can meditate on God.

Guard your heart above all else, for it determines the course of your life.   PROVERBS 4:23

I wait quietly before God, for my victory comes from him. . . . Let all that I am wait quietly before God, for my hope is in him. . . . Pour out your heart to him, for God is our refuge.   PSALM 62:1, 5, 8

*Q*uiet times are necessary for fighting temptation. The best time to prepare for temptation is before it hits you. Train yourself in your quiet times so that you will have the spiritual wisdom, strength, and commitment to honor God in the face of temptation.

Then I will win her back once again. I will lead her into the desert and speak tenderly to her there.

HOSEA 2:14

*G*od pursues you by leading and guiding you—sometimes to secluded, quiet, out-of-*your*-way places.

DIVINE CHALLENGE

CLOTHE YOURSELVES INSTEAD WITH THE BEAUTY THAT COMES FROM WITHIN, THE UNFADING BEAUTY OF A GENTLE AND QUIET SPIRIT, WHICH IS SO PRECIOUS TO GOD.

1 Peter 3:4

Quitting

MY QUESTION *for* GOD

How do I know when I should keep going or when it's time to quit?

A MOMENT *with* GOD

Think carefully about what is right, and stop sinning.

1 CORINTHIANS 15:34

Be strong and courageous, and do the work. Don't be afraid or discouraged, for the LORD God, my God, is with you. He will not fail you or forsake you. He will see to it that all the work . . . is finished correctly.

1 CHRONICLES 28:20

Do not let sin control the way you live; do not give in
to sinful desires.   ROMANS 6:12

We are pressed on every side by troubles, but we are
not crushed. We are perplexed, but not driven to
despair. . . . We know that God, who raised the Lord
Jesus, will also raise us with Jesus and present us to
himself together with you. . . . That is why we never
give up.   2 CORINTHIANS 4:8, 14, 16

It is time to quit when you are doing something
wrong, when your actions are futile, or when you are
hurting yourself or others. Even if what you are doing
is not inherently wrong, it may be time to quit if that
action or behavior is not productive, absorbs too much
of your time and attention, or is a stumbling block to
others. However, when God has called you to a task,
you should not give up. Not only would you miss the
great blessings of reaching your goal, but you might
also bring discipline upon yourself for not trusting God
to help you get there. Just because God wants you to
do something doesn't mean it will be easy. In fact, the
harder the task, the more important it often is. If you
know God is asking you to do something in particular
or if he is taking you in a new certain direction, don't
give up just because the going gets tough. If anything,
that should tell you that you are headed in the right
direction. Keep moving forward boldly and faithfully.

DIVINE PROMISE

LET'S NOT GET TIRED OF DOING WHAT IS
GOOD. AT JUST THE RIGHT TIME WE WILL REAP
A HARVEST OF BLESSING IF WE DON'T GIVE UP.
Galatians 6:9

Reconciliation

MY QUESTION *for* GOD

Why is reconciliation important for effective leadership?

A MOMENT *with* GOD

If you are presenting a sacrifice at the altar in the
Temple and you suddenly remember that someone has
something against you, leave your sacrifice there at
the altar. Go and be reconciled to that person. Then
come and offer your sacrifice to God.   MATTHEW 5:23-24

Make allowance for each other's faults, and forgive
anyone who offends you. Remember, the Lord
forgave you, so you must forgive others.   COLOSSIANS 3:13

If another believer sins against you, go privately and
point out the offense. If the other person listens and
confesses it, you have won that person back.

MATTHEW 18:15

*R*econciliation is at the heart of the story of God and
humankind. Ever since sin entered the world, God has
been pursuing all people in order to reconcile each person

with himself. He sent his Son, Jesus, to suffer the agony of the cross so that sinful human beings could be forgiven and therefore be reconciled to him, the Holy One. Jesus taught that our reconciliation with God is to produce reconciliation with others. Reconciliation in human relationships is so important that Jesus commands us even to interrupt our worship in order to first be reconciled to the people in our lives with whom we may have conflict. To live with an unresolved human conflict actually hinders our relationship with God. Leaders are often involved in conflict, and sometimes it seems impossible to resolve it. But reconciling with other people is important to God because it demonstrates a humble and forgiving spirit, which is essential to healthy relationships. And healthy relationships are essential to effective leadership. Reconciliation becomes possible only when someone makes the first move: a hand extended, a phone call, a word spoken in forgiveness. If there is anyone in your life with whom you need to pursue reconciliation, follow Jesus' advice and go to that person right away so the relationship can be restored.

DIVINE PROMISE

"MY WAYWARD CHILDREN," SAYS THE LORD, "COME BACK TO ME, AND I WILL HEAL YOUR WAYWARD HEARTS." "YES, WE'RE COMING," THE PEOPLE REPLY, "FOR YOU ARE THE LORD OUR GOD." *Jeremiah 3:22*

Regrets

MY QUESTION *for* GOD

*There are so many things I regret doing. How do I get over
my regrets?*

A MOMENT *with* GOD

Peter was sitting outside in the courtyard. A servant
girl came over and said to him, "You were one of
those with Jesus the Galilean." But Peter denied
it in front of everyone. "I don't know what you're
talking about," he said. Later, out by the gate, another
servant girl noticed him and said to those standing
around, "This man was with Jesus of Nazareth."
Again Peter denied it, this time with an oath. "I
don't even know the man," he said. A little later
some of the other bystanders came over to Peter and
said, "You must be one of them; we can tell by your
Galilean accent." Peter swore, "A curse on me if I'm
lying—I don't know the man!" And immediately
the rooster crowed. Suddenly, Jesus' words flashed
through Peter's mind: "Before the rooster crows, you
will deny three times that you even know me." And
he went away, weeping bitterly.   MATTHEW 26:69-75

Now I say to you that you are Peter (which means
"rock"), and upon this rock I will build my church, and
all the powers of hell will not conquer it.   MATTHEW 16:18

This means that anyone who belongs to Christ has
become a new person. The old life is gone; a new life
has begun!   2 CORINTHIANS 5:17

If the memories and experiences of your life were compared to rocks that you have collected and must carry in a backpack, surely guilt and regret would be among the heaviest. Guilt is a legitimate spiritual response to sin. Regret is sorrow over the consequences of your decisions, both the sinful and the simply unfortunate. While God promises to remove the guilt of all who seek his forgiveness, he does not prevent the consequences of your sin. It is likely the regret over those consequences that you are carrying, and it weighs you down with remorse. God promises to help you deal with your regrets so you can move on to the future without carrying a heavy load of guilt. When you sincerely ask God for forgiveness, he promises to forget the past, and he gives you a fresh start. You still have to live with the consequences of your actions, because those cannot be retracted. But because God forgives and forgets, you can move forward without the heavy burden of regret. Because God no longer holds your past against you, you no longer need to hold it against yourself. You can be free from self-condemnation. It is a divine moment when you truly grasp the power of God's healing forgiveness and are able to turn your regrets into resolve. Regrets can be so enslaving that they consume your thoughts and disable you from serving God in the future. If Peter had focused on the regret he experienced after denying Jesus, he would never have been able to preach the Good News so powerfully. Don't let regret paralyze your desire or your ability to lead. Instead, let God's forgiveness motivate you to positive action for him in the future.

DIVINE PROMISE

DAVID ALSO SPOKE OF THIS WHEN HE
DESCRIBED THE HAPPINESS OF THOSE WHO
ARE DECLARED RIGHTEOUS WITHOUT
WORKING FOR IT: "OH, WHAT JOY FOR THOSE
WHOSE DISOBEDIENCE IS FORGIVEN, WHOSE
SINS ARE PUT OUT OF SIGHT. YES, WHAT JOY
FOR THOSE WHOSE RECORD THE LORD HAS
CLEARED OF SIN."   *Romans 4:6-8*

Remembering

MY QUESTION *for* GOD

How can the act of remembering help me in my spiritual walk?

A MOMENT *with* GOD

For I, the LORD, am the one who brought you up
from the land of Egypt, that I might be your God.
Therefore, you must be holy because I am holy.

LEVITICUS 11:45

I lie awake thinking of you, meditating on you
through the night.   PSALM 63:6

That is the time to be careful! Beware that in your
plenty you do not forget the LORD your God and
disobey his commands, regulations, and decrees that
I am giving you today. . . . Do not become proud
at that time and forget the LORD your God, who
rescued you from slavery in the land of Egypt.

DEUTERONOMY 8:11, 14

Remember the days of long ago; think about the generations past. Ask your father, and he will inform you. Inquire of your elders, and they will tell you.

DEUTERONOMY 32:7

When I see the rainbow in the clouds, I will remember the eternal covenant between God and every living creature on earth.

GENESIS 9:16

*M*any times God reminded the Israelites that he was the one who rescued them from Egypt. Why was it important to keep reminding them? God is the one who helps fight and win life's battles. Remembering how he has helped you in the past gives you hope and confidence that he will help you in the future, especially when it seems as if no human solution is possible. Remembering the miracles of God reminds you of his divine nature and helps you notice the divine moments when he breaks into your life in a special way. When you have lost hope, think back to God's previous work in your life. When you recount God's past faithfulness before others, it can be an act of worship. It can also introduce an unbeliever to the greatness of your God. If you can't think of any ways God has worked for you in the past, remember God's greatest work in you—the work of your salvation. That is the greatest miracle of all.

WE WILL NOT HIDE THESE TRUTHS FROM
OUR CHILDREN; WE WILL TELL THE NEXT
GENERATION ABOUT THE GLORIOUS DEEDS
OF THE LORD, ABOUT HIS POWER AND HIS
MIGHTY WONDERS.   *Psalm 78:4*

Repentance

MY QUESTION *for* GOD

Why is repentance important for effective leadership?

A MOMENT *with* GOD

You confessed, "We have sinned against the LORD!
We will go into the land and fight for it, as the LORD
our God has commanded us." So your men strapped
on their weapons, thinking it would be easy to
attack the hill country. But the LORD told me to tell
you, "Do not attack, for I am not with you. If you
go ahead on your own, you will be crushed by your
enemies." This is what I told you, but you would not
listen. Instead, you again rebelled against the LORD's
command and arrogantly went into the hill country
to fight.   DEUTERONOMY 1:41-43

Repentance is motivated by the realization that you
have done something wrong in the way you are living
and treating others. The Bible calls this sin. Repentance
means you admit your sin and make a commitment, with
God's help, to change your life's direction. While it is

not a popular concept these days, repentance is essential because it is the only way to arrive at the two most important destinations: where God wants to lead you here on earth, and where he ultimately wants you to end up—heaven. Because of repentance, change is possible. You can experience God's fullest blessings both now and for eternity. Repentance is that divine moment when you decide to move toward God instead of away from him. For repentance to occur, you must tell God you are truly sorry for your sin, and you must commit to turning away from your sin and living in obedience to God. In the verses above, the Israelites confessed their sin, but they didn't really mean it. They seemed to be saying, "Oh, sorry about that. Now let's get on with the conquest of the land." Apathetic repentance is not repentance at all. When you repent, you must truly be sorry and committed to change. You must also realize that even though you have repented, the consequences have already been set in motion. God was not going to allow the Israelites into the Promised Land at this particular point; their sin had prevented that. By refusing to submit to God's discipline, they proved God's point that their repentance wasn't genuine. Repentance is demonstrated by change, and it is through confession and forgiveness that you experience real change.

DIVINE PROMISE

IF MY PEOPLE WHO ARE CALLED BY MY NAME
WILL HUMBLE THEMSELVES AND PRAY AND
SEEK MY FACE AND TURN FROM THEIR WICKED
WAYS, I WILL HEAR FROM HEAVEN AND WILL
FORGIVE THEIR SINS.   *2 Chronicles 7:14*

Reputation

MY QUESTION *for* GOD

How important is a good reputation?

A MOMENT *with* GOD

"Here I am, a stranger and a foreigner among you. Please sell me a piece of land so I can give my wife a proper burial." The Hittites replied to Abraham, "Listen, my lord, you are an honored prince among us. Choose the finest of our tombs and bury her there. No one here will refuse to help you in this way." GENESIS 23:4-6

$\mathcal{L}$ike it or not, you already have a reputation. Whether you intentionally try to project a certain image or you couldn't care less what others think, people form an opinion of you based on what you do and say. Abraham's reputation earned him respect even among strangers. A life invested in obedience to God results in a reputation that brings honor and respect. Reputation is the yardstick others use to measure your character—the real you. Take a moment to imagine what others might be saying about you. Carefully consider what your reputation is built upon.

DIVINE PROMISE

CHOOSE A GOOD REPUTATION OVER GREAT RICHES; BEING HELD IN HIGH ESTEEM IS BETTER THAN SILVER OR GOLD. *Proverbs 22:1*

Respect

MY QUESTION *for* GOD

How can I show respect to other leaders?

A MOMENT *with* GOD

Honor those who are your leaders in the Lord's work.
. . . Show them great respect and wholehearted love
because of their work.   1 THESSALONIANS 5:12-13

They stood on each side of Moses, holding up his
hands. So his hands held steady until sunset.

EXODUS 17:12

*E*ncourage them. Those who lead can become discouraged. Show your support and respect not only
with words but also with actions.

Pray for us. . . . Especially pray that I will be able to
come back to you soon.   HEBREWS 13:18-19

*P*ray for them. Leaders need other people interceding
on their behalf. Perhaps the best way to support leaders
is to pray for God's care and protection for them.

Why do you condemn another believer? Why do you
look down on another believer? Remember, we will all
stand before the judgment seat of God.   ROMANS 14:10

Be slow to criticize. If you think a leader has done something wrong, confront him or her privately. Don't be hasty to ruin someone's reputation; that only gives you a reputation as a gossip and a slanderer.

Then Nathan said to David, "You are that man! The LORD, the God of Israel, says: I anointed you king of Israel and saved you from the power of Saul. . . . And if that had not been enough, I would have given you much, much more. Why, then, have you despised the word of the LORD and done this horrible deed? For you have murdered Uriah the Hittite . . . and stolen his wife."   2 SAMUEL 12:7-9

Hold them accountable. Leaders need the support and advice of others. Everyone makes mistakes, and leaders need trusted friends and advisers to help them avoid costly mistakes and maintain a lifestyle of integrity.

DIVINE CHALLENGE

HONOR THOSE WHO ARE YOUR LEADERS IN THE LORD'S WORK.   *1 Thessalonians 5:12*

Responsibility

MY QUESTION *for* GOD

Why do I need to take responsibility for my actions?

A MOMENT *with* GOD

It was the woman you gave me who gave me the fruit, and I ate it.   GENESIS 3:12

[Pilate] sent for a bowl of water and washed his hands before the crowd, saying, "I am innocent of this man's blood. The responsibility is yours!"   MATTHEW 27:24

Don't excuse yourself by saying, "Look, we didn't know." For God understands all hearts, and he sees you. He who guards your soul knows you knew.

PROVERBS 24:12

*W*hen God confronted Adam for his sin, Adam's first response was to blame Eve. Pilate tried to deflect responsibility for sentencing Jesus to death. Unfortunately, that is often the pattern in our world. Few people take responsibility for their own actions; they prefer to blame someone or something else. God says that we are responsible for our own conduct. Be courageous—take responsibility for yourself and your actions. You will be more motivated to do what is right, and you will win the respect of others.

DIVINE PROMISE

THE LORD WILL WITHHOLD NO GOOD THING FROM THOSE WHO DO WHAT IS RIGHT.

Psalm 84:11

Rest

MY QUESTION *for* GOD

Why is rest important?

A MOMENT *with* GOD

So the creation of the heavens and the earth and everything in them was completed. On the seventh day God had finished his work of creation, so he rested from all his work. And God blessed the seventh day and declared it holy, because it was the day when he rested from all his work of creation.   GENESIS 2:1-3

It is a permanent sign of my covenant with the people of Israel. For in six days the LORD made heaven and earth, but on the seventh day he stopped working and was refreshed.   EXODUS 31:17

The LORD is my shepherd; I have all that I need. He lets me rest in green meadows; he leads me beside peaceful streams. He renews my strength. He guides me along right paths, bringing honor to his name.

PSALM 23:1-3

It is useless for you to work so hard from early morning until late at night, anxiously working for food to eat; for God gives rest to his loved ones.   PSALM 127:2

*T*oday we often experience anxiety and stress because we live in an age of perpetual motion. We take pride in explaining to each other how busy we are, and we feel vaguely guilty when we relax. God did not intend for his people to live in a state of frenzied activity. From God's own example in Genesis to the promises he makes in the New Testament, it is clear that God wants us to discover rest and refreshment for body and soul. Why did the omnipotent God of the universe rest following his work of creation? Surely it wasn't because the Almighty was physically tired! The answer is that God, in ceasing from his work, proclaimed his rest to be holy. God knew that his people would need to cease their work to care for their physical and spiritual needs. Work is good, but it must be balanced with regular rest and attention to the health of your soul. Otherwise, you might miss the divine moments God sends your way. Make sure to carve out regular times of rest for worship and spiritual refreshment.

DIVINE PROMISE

COME TO ME, ALL OF YOU WHO ARE WEARY AND CARRY HEAVY BURDENS, AND I WILL GIVE YOU REST. *Matthew 11:28*

Retirement

MY QUESTION *for* GOD

What does the Bible say about retirement?

A Moment *with* God

The Lord also instructed Moses, "This is the rule
the Levites must follow: They must begin serving
in the Tabernacle at the age of twenty-five, and they
must retire at the age of fifty. After retirement they
may assist their fellow Levites by serving as guards
at the Tabernacle, but they may not officiate in
the service."   Numbers 8:23-26

He makes the whole body fit together perfectly. As
each part does its own special work, it helps the other
parts grow, so that the whole body is healthy and
growing and full of love.   Ephesians 4:16

The Levites were officially assigned to serve God in
the Tabernacle from age twenty-five to fifty. At age
fifty, they were required to retire. They could still assist other Levites in active duties, but they could not officiate in the service. We should not assume the Bible is
suggesting that fifty is the age all workers should retire!
This is one of the few references to retirement in the
Bible. God may have commanded it to encourage the
younger Levites to grow into positions of responsibility. It was important for this new nation to have plenty
of strong leaders. Nowhere does the Bible say that retirement means stopping work and service altogether.
Rather, retirement brings a change in how we work
and serve. There are few things more important than
developing strong leaders in the church, and sometimes
older leaders must shift from leading to mentoring new
leaders for the future strength of the church.

DIVINE PROMISE

AMONG YOU IT WILL BE DIFFERENT. WHOEVER
WANTS TO BE A LEADER AMONG YOU MUST
BE YOUR SERVANT. AND WHOEVER WANTS TO
BE FIRST AMONG YOU MUST BE THE SLAVE OF
EVERYONE ELSE.   *Mark 10:43-44*

Right

MY QUESTION *for* GOD

How do leaders stand up for what is right?

A MOMENT *with* GOD

The Israelites did not attack the towns, for the
Israelite leaders had made a vow to them in the name
of the LORD, the God of Israel. The people of Israel
grumbled against their leaders because of the treaty.
But the leaders replied, "Since we have sworn an oath
in the presence of the LORD, the God of Israel, we
cannot touch them. This is what we must do. We
must let them live, for divine anger would come upon
us if we broke our oath."   JOSHUA 9:18-20

One of the responsibilities of a good leader is to promote the best interests of his or her people, as long
as those interests are consistent with God's Word.
Joshua and his leadership team made a terrible mistake in signing this peace treaty, but they had to keep
their promise. The people grumbled against them. As

the pressure mounted, so did the temptation to bow to politics—if the majority of people wanted to annul the treaty, then they should do it. Good leaders want what's best for their people, but they also realize that what is best should always be consistent with what is right. When what is right is a minority opinion, it takes true courage for a leader to stand with firm resolve and help the people see that what is right also leads them in the right direction. Consistently doing what is right and keeping your promises make you a leader who can be trusted.

DIVINE PROMISE

THE LORD REWARDED ME FOR DOING RIGHT.
HE HAS SEEN MY INNOCENCE. TO THE
FAITHFUL YOU SHOW YOURSELF FAITHFUL;
TO THOSE WITH INTEGRITY YOU SHOW
INTEGRITY.   *Psalm 18:24-25*

Risk

MY QUESTION *for* GOD

What principles should I keep in mind when assessing risks?

A MOMENT *with* GOD

Those who trust their own insight are foolish, but anyone who walks in wisdom is safe.   PROVERBS 28:26

Fools think their own way is right, but the wise listen to others.
                                                              PROVERBS 12:15

Fools base their thoughts on foolish assumptions, so their conclusions will be wicked madness.
                                                              ECCLESIASTES 10:13

*T*here is a difference between being a risk-taker and being a fool. The Bible warns us not to take risks that ignore or contradict sound principles. Consulting God and wise, godly friends before taking action provides a higher chance of success. Fools rarely consult others, they never consult God, and they make plans that are mostly for personal gain. God looks for wise and obedient risk-takers, not foolish people who plunge ahead without first seeking his guidance.

The LORD said to Joshua, "Do not be afraid or discouraged."
                                                              JOSHUA 8:1

Be strong and courageous, and do the work. Don't be afraid or discouraged, for the LORD God, my God, is with you. He will not fail you or forsake you. He will see to it that all the work . . . is finished correctly.
                                                              1 CHRONICLES 28:20

*D*on't be afraid to risk failure. The only true failure is that which utterly defeats you and makes you unable to try again. Joshua was defeated at the battle of Ai. He dealt with the causes of defeat head-on, then led his army out once again into battle, and they won a great victory. You must have the courage to face failure and take risks again. The lessons you learn from your failures will make you better able to assess risks in the future. If you don't give up, yesterday's failure can become tomorrow's victory.

DIVINE PROMISE

JESUS TOLD HIM, "YOU BELIEVE BECAUSE YOU HAVE SEEN ME. BLESSED ARE THOSE WHO BELIEVE WITHOUT SEEING ME." *John 20:29*

Self-Control

MY QUESTION *for* GOD

Self-control is so hard to develop. Why is it important?

A MOMENT *with* GOD

I have discovered this principle of life—that when I want to do what is right, I inevitably do what is wrong. I love God's law with all my heart. But there is another power within me that is at war with my mind. This power makes me a slave to the sin that is still within me. Oh, what a miserable person I am! Who will free me from this life that is dominated by sin and death? Thank God! The answer is in Jesus Christ our Lord. So you see how it is: In my mind I really want to obey God's law, but because of my sinful nature I am a slave to sin.   ROMANS 7:21-25

Supplement your faith with a generous provision
of moral excellence, and moral excellence with
knowledge, and knowledge with self-control, and
self-control with patient endurance, and patient
endurance with godliness.   2 PETER 1:5-6

Train yourself to be godly. Physical training is good,
but training for godliness is much better, promising
benefits in this life and in the life to come.

                                    1 TIMOTHY 4:7-8

*S*elf-control is one of the hardest character traits to
achieve because it means denying what comes natu-
rally to your sinful nature and replacing it with a controlled, godly response. When you are trying to lead
other people, with all their problems and flaws, this
becomes all the more difficult. Gaining self-control
is a lifelong endeavor; just when you think you have
one area of your life mastered, another area gets out of
control. Some of the hardest things to control are your
thoughts, your words, and your physical appetites. It
is only with the divine help of the Holy Spirit that you
can achieve the kind of self-control that allows you to
become a consistent and effective leader. Only then
will you have the discipline to keep bad habits and sinful tendencies from tripping you up so you can remain
focused on your goals and the purposes for which God
placed you in leadership.

DIVINE PROMISE

THE HOLY SPIRIT PRODUCES THIS KIND OF FRUIT IN OUR LIVES: LOVE, JOY, PEACE . . . AND SELF-CONTROL.   *Galatians 5:22-23*

Service

MY QUESTION *for* GOD

What does it mean to be a servant leader?

A MOMENT *with* GOD

Though he was God, he did not think of equality with God as something to cling to. . . . In human form, he humbled himself.   PHILIPPIANS 2:6-8

*J*esus revolutionized our understanding of leadership by teaching "downward mobility." In a striking picture of servanthood, Jesus humbled himself by performing the task of a slave. Jesus' obedience to his Father's will modeled how far we are to go in serving others.

When Jesus heard them, he stopped and called, "What do you want me to do for you?"   MATTHEW 20:32

*B*eing a servant leader means listening and responding to the needs of those around you.

He got up from the table, took off his robe, wrapped a towel around his waist, and poured water into a

basin. Then he began to wash the disciples' feet,
drying them with the towel he had around him.

JOHN 13:4-5

*A*s a servant leader, you should be willing to perform
any task that you delegate to others.

Mary responded, "I am the Lord's servant. May
everything you have said about me come true." And
then the angel left her.

LUKE 1:38

*T*he essence of servant leadership is humbly doing
what God asks you to do.

If you do not carry your own cross and follow me,
you cannot be my disciple.

LUKE 14:27

*Y*ou must learn to follow God before you can learn
to lead.

DIVINE CHALLENGE

WHOEVER WANTS TO BE A LEADER AMONG
YOU MUST BE YOUR SERVANT, AND WHOEVER
WANTS TO BE FIRST AMONG YOU MUST BE THE
SLAVE OF EVERYONE ELSE. *Mark 10:43-44*

Sin

MY QUESTION *for* GOD

Do my "little" sins matter as long as I am accomplishing good things overall?

A MOMENT *with* GOD

You used to live in sin, just like the rest of the world.

EPHESIANS 2:2

You will always harvest what you plant.   GALATIANS 6:7

Listen! The LORD's arm is not too weak to save you, nor is his ear too deaf to hear you call. It's your sins that have cut you off from God.   ISAIAH 59:1-2

Remember, it is sin to know what you ought to do and then not do it.   JAMES 4:17

When you follow the desires of your sinful nature, the results are very clear: . . . impurity . . . hostility, quarreling, jealousy, outbursts of anger, selfish ambition, dissension, division, envy, drunkenness.

GALATIANS 5:19-21

You may be sure that your sin will find you out.

NUMBERS 32:23

*A*s leaders, it's sometimes tempting to overlook the "little" sins in yourself and others to keep the peace or advance the cause. It might be a telling a little white lie that helps seal the deal, leaving out some key negative facts at a presentation, looking the other way when an employee exaggerates the data, or using foul language that is inappropriate for a Christian. Sometimes you do something wrong and do not even realize it until later. Your business might accidentally break a city ordinance, or the IRS might call you on a tax loophole you innocently claimed. In the laws of government, ignorance is no excuse for breaking the law. So it is with God's law. To God, sin is sin, whether it is small or even unintentional. All sin has consequences, but small, intentional sins can eat away at your integrity until eventually your conscience becomes desensitized and no longer recognizes what you are doing as sin. To recognize all sin as sin is a divine moment that will keep you on the path of integrity and help you stay close to God. You need to regularly check up on yourself so that sins do not go unchecked and their consequences become disastrous.

DIVINE CHALLENGE
DO NOT LET SIN CONTROL THE WAY YOU LIVE.
Romans 6:12

MY QUESTION *for* GOD
How do I handle persistent, stubborn sin?

A MOMENT *with* GOD

I myself, as well as my brothers and my workers, have been lending the people money and grain, but now let us stop this business of charging interest. NEHEMIAH 5:10

*P*eople can be stubborn, but so can sin. Stubborn sins are deeply rooted sinful habits that we just can't seem to shake—and don't really want to. We all have them, and we keep them hidden as much as we can, but they still distract us. Because sin is often disguised as desirable or harmless, we don't want to give up the ones that give us pleasure. We like the way they make us feel. That's why these are stubborn sins—their roots have grown deep down inside us. Greed was one of those stubborn sins affecting several of the wealthy lenders in Nehemiah's day. They were charging exorbitant interest rates and creating a class of poor people. Instead of setting a ceiling of maximum interest rates, Nehemiah banned interest-bearing loans altogether. And this decree affected Nehemiah personally. He had been lending money and grain, undoubtedly at a just rate of return, but he was willing to give it up in order to root out the abuses connected with making loans. This passage isn't teaching that it's wrong to charge interest on loans, but it is pointing to several key principles for defeating the stubborn sins that will sooner or later affect your Christian influence: (1) Make a clean break; a gradual withdrawal from your sinful habit won't be effective. (2) As much as possible, avoid any situation that will tempt you in that area of weakness. (3) Do whatever it takes to help your Christian brothers and sisters live by God's standards, even if it is personally inconvenient for you. You might have to make a lifestyle sacrifice for the good of those you lead, but deeply rooted sin must be pulled out altogether, not simply pruned.

DIVINE CHALLENGE

SEARCH ME, O GOD, AND KNOW MY HEART; TEST ME AND KNOW MY ANXIOUS THOUGHTS. POINT OUT ANYTHING IN ME THAT OFFENDS YOU, AND LEAD ME ALONG THE PATH OF EVERLASTING LIFE.   *Psalm 139:23-24*

Solutions

MY QUESTION *for* GOD

How do I find the right solutions to my problems?

A MOMENT *with* GOD

Now Sarai, Abram's wife, had not been able to bear children for him. But she had an Egyptian servant named Hagar. So Sarai said to Abram, "The LORD has prevented me from having children. Go and sleep with my servant. Perhaps I can have children through her." And Abram agreed with Sarai's proposal. So Sarai, Abram's wife, took Hagar the Egyptian servant and gave her to Abram as a wife. . . . So Abram had sexual relations with Hagar, and she became pregnant. But when Hagar knew she was pregnant, she began to treat her mistress, Sarai, with contempt.

Then Sarai said to Abram, "This is all your fault! I put my servant into your arms, but now that she's pregnant she treats me with contempt. The LORD will show who's wrong—you or me!" Abram replied, "Look, she is your servant, so deal with her as you see fit." Then Sarai treated Hagar so harshly that she finally ran away. GENESIS 16:1-6

*S*arai blamed Abram for the results of her arrangement to use Hagar to gain the child that God had promised. We tend to blame others for our self-inflicted problems that often result from our own poor solutions. When you make a mistake, don't make a bigger one by blaming someone else. This only causes a rift in the relationship. Abram didn't want to deal with the problem when Sarai came to him to discuss it, so he simply sidestepped it. He could have stepped in and helped Hagar. Avoiding problems, particularly those you helped to create, only makes them worse, and it often hurts those who were innocently sucked in to the mess you created. Acknowledging and dealing with your mistake is embarrassing and sometimes even humiliating, but it is the only way to find a solution to the problem and restore the respect you need to continue to lead effectively.

DIVINE PROMISE

GOD BLESSES THOSE WHO WORK FOR PEACE, FOR THEY WILL BE CALLED THE CHILDREN OF GOD. *Matthew 5:9*

Sorrow

MY QUESTION for GOD

What can I do when sorrow overwhelms me?

A MOMENT with GOD

[Elijah] went on alone into the wilderness, traveling
all day. He sat down under a solitary broom tree
and prayed that he might die. "I have had enough,
LORD," he said. "Take my life, for I am no better than
my ancestors who have already died." Then he lay
down and slept under the broom tree. But as he was
sleeping, an angel touched him and told him, "Get
up and eat!" He looked around and there beside his
head was some bread baked on hot stones and a jar of
water! So he ate and drank and lay down again.

1 KINGS 19:4-6

Look! He has placed the land in front of you. Go and
occupy it as the LORD, the God of your ancestors, has
promised you. Don't be afraid! Don't be discouraged!

DEUTERONOMY 1:21

Let's not get tired of doing what is good. At just the
right time we will reap a harvest of blessing if we
don't give up.

GALATIANS 6:9

This is what the LORD of Heaven's Armies says:
"All this may seem impossible to you now, a small
remnant of God's people. But is it impossible
for me?"

ZECHARIAH 8:6

$\mathcal{L}$eaders are not immune to sorrow. In fact, as a leader you will deal not just with your own sorrow but with the sorrow of all those you lead. It can be overwhelming. Recovery from deep sorrow involves a number of factors, including a new perspective. Elijah was tired, hungry, and feeling completely alone. A period of rest, physical refreshment, and engagement with God helped him to regain a proper perspective and reconnect with God's purpose for his life. Sorrow over a loss is natural and appropriate because it helps you process grief. But if sorrow is allowed to linger too long, it can lead to depression. You lose the hope God offers you and the big picture of God's purpose for you. If you are still overwhelmed by sorrow after a period of grieving and rest, a wise counselor can help you regain a healthy perspective. Rest is restorative and advice is healing, but leaders too often neglect these important avenues of help. Left unchecked, sorrow can cause you to turn inward and become paralyzed by your sadness and pain. It takes effort, but you need to focus your attention outward, on God. Every day he opens doors of opportunity that can bring purpose and meaning to you: helping someone in need, volunteering for a good cause, writing a note of encouragement to someone else who needs it. When you look up from your own sorrow, you will see the door God has opened for you. Walk through it with courage, and on the other side you will begin to find relief.

DIVINE PROMISE

HE WILL WIPE EVERY TEAR FROM THEIR EYES,
AND THERE WILL BE NO MORE DEATH OR
SORROW OR CRYING OR PAIN. ALL THESE
THINGS ARE GONE FOREVER.   *Revelation 21:4*

Spiritual Disciplines

MY QUESTION *for* GOD

How can I keep my heart in tune with God's heart?

A MOMENT *with* GOD

Guard your heart above all else, for it determines the
course of your life.   PROVERBS 4:23

Every aspect of life is affected by the spiritual condition of your heart. Because of the impact a leader
can make on others, you must care for your inner life.
Otherwise, your weakness, wounds, and weariness
will likely affect those around you in negative ways.
Likewise, spiritual vitality will inspire and sustain
those around you. The spiritual disciplines (such as
meditation, prayer, fasting, and Bible study) are some
ways you can care for your heart and soul. They are not
practiced to impress God, but rather to allow God to
impress himself on you so that you in turn can make
an impact on others. They are not achievements you
perform for God but ways you make yourself available
to him.

Don't you realize that in a race everyone runs, but only one person gets the prize? So run to win! All athletes are disciplined in their training. They do it to win a prize that will fade away, but we do it for an eternal prize. So I run with purpose in every step. I am not just shadowboxing. I discipline my body like an athlete, training it to do what it should. Otherwise, I fear that after preaching to others I myself might be disqualified.   1 CORINTHIANS 9:24-27

An athlete trains over and over again so that fundamental skills become automatic. In the same way, spiritual disciplines can be practiced so that following God faithfully is an automatic reflex that will guard your heart when anything tries to tempt or attack it.

When you come to worship me, who asked you to parade through my courts with all your ceremony? Stop bringing me your meaningless gifts; the incense of your offerings disgusts me! As for your celebrations . . . and your special days for fasting— they are all sinful and false . . . for your hands are covered with the blood of innocent victims. Wash yourselves and be clean! Get your sins out of my sight. Give up your evil ways. Learn to do good. Seek justice. Help the oppressed. Defend the cause of orphans. Fight for the rights of widows.   ISAIAH 1:12-17

It's important to remember that the spiritual disciplines cannot take the place of a heart committed to

God. They become mere hypocrisy when they are not motivated by a sincere desire for God and his will in your life.

DIVINE PROMISE

DON'T WORRY ABOUT ANYTHING; INSTEAD, PRAY ABOUT EVERYTHING. TELL GOD WHAT YOU NEED, AND THANK HIM FOR ALL HE HAS DONE. THEN YOU WILL EXPERIENCE GOD'S PEACE, WHICH EXCEEDS ANYTHING WE CAN UNDERSTAND. HIS PEACE WILL GUARD YOUR HEARTS AND MINDS AS YOU LIVE IN CHRIST JESUS. *Philippians 4:6-7*

Spiritual Dryness

MY QUESTIONS *for* GOD

What do I do when I feel spiritually dry? How do I maintain my enthusiasm for serving God?

A MOMENT *with* GOD

The seed on the rocky soil represents those who hear the message and immediately receive it with joy. But since they don't have deep roots, they don't last long. They fall away as soon as they have problems or are persecuted for believing God's word. MATTHEW 13:20-21

You must warn each other every day, while it is still "today," so that none of you will be deceived by sin and hardened against God. HEBREWS 3:13

If you give even a cup of cold water to one of the least
of my followers, you will surely be rewarded.

Matthew 10:42

*S*corching temperatures, blazing sun, and days without rain result in drought. Plants wilt, streams dry
up, everything is thirsty. We can all relate to feeling
parched in the dry heat, longing for a drink of cold
water. Our souls can become dry, too, thirsting for
something that will truly refresh and satisfy. Seasons
of drought come in your spiritual life when you experience the blazing pressures of the world or the heat of
temptation. Your desire to be close to God and serve
him dries up. Your enthusiasm for leading can dry up
too. You're not growing in your faith, and you're not
sure if you want to. Just as a farmer must take extra
care of the fields during a drought, so you must take
extra care of your soul during times of spiritual dry-
ness, watering it with God's Word and reviving it with
renewed purpose. Just as God sends the rains to refresh
the earth, he also sends divine moments to revive your
passion and purpose for him. He alone quenches your
spiritual thirst. When you see the chance to refresh
your soul, act immediately before the drought causes
unnecessary damage to your faith. Often these moments come as opportunities to join others in acts of
service. When you give a cup of cold water to someone
in need (see Matthew 10:42), your thirst is quenched
as well, and your enthusiasm for God is refreshed.

DIVINE PROMISE
THE LORD WILL GUIDE YOU CONTINUALLY,
GIVING YOU WATER WHEN YOU ARE DRY
AND RESTORING YOUR STRENGTH. YOU WILL
BE LIKE A WELL-WATERED GARDEN, LIKE AN
EVER-FLOWING SPRING.   *Isaiah 58:11*

Spiritual Gifts

MY QUESTION *for* GOD
How do spiritual gifts make me available for God's use?

A MOMENT *with* GOD

A spiritual gift is given to each of us so we can help
each other. To one person the Spirit gives the ability
to give wise advice; to another the same Spirit gives a
message of special knowledge. The same Spirit gives
great faith to another, and to someone else the one
Spirit gives the gift of healing. . . . In fact, some parts
of the body that seem weakest and least important are
actually the most necessary.   1 CORINTHIANS 12:7-9, 22

God has given each of you a gift from his great variety
of spiritual gifts. Use them well to serve one another.

1 PETER 4:10

I heard the LORD asking, "Whom should I send as a
messenger to this people? Who will go for us?" I said,
"Here I am. Send me."   ISAIAH 6:8

*B*eing available for God to use you includes the continual development of the gifts he has given you. Then you will be prepared to serve him. You must be willing to use your unique gifts to serve God in the calling he currently has for you. Leaders must discover their spiritual gifts in order to be the most effective in influencing others. If you don't know your spiritual gifts, take a spiritual-gifts assessment or ask your friends what they think your gifts are. God gives each individual a spiritual gift (sometimes more than one!) and special opportunities to use those gifts to help and encourage others. Using your gifts fulfills the purpose for which God made you. You can never use up these spiritual gifts; rather, the more you use them, the more they grow and help you make a unique contribution within your sphere of influence. Using your spiritual gifts gives you many divine moments when you find the sweet spot of your effectiveness for God.

DIVINE PROMISE

THIS IS WHY I REMIND YOU TO FAN INTO FLAMES THE SPIRITUAL GIFT GOD GAVE YOU WHEN I LAID MY HANDS ON YOU. FOR GOD HAS NOT GIVEN US A SPIRIT OF FEAR AND TIMIDITY, BUT OF POWER, LOVE, AND SELF-DISCIPLINE. *2 Timothy 1:6-7*

Spiritual Warfare

MY QUESTION *for* GOD

How do I fight spiritual battles?

A MOMENT *with* GOD

Stay alert! Watch out for your great enemy, the devil. He prowls around like a roaring lion, looking for someone to devour. Stand firm against him, and be strong in your faith.

1 PETER 5:8-9

The devil . . . was a murderer from the beginning. He has always hated the truth, because there is no truth in him. When he lies, it is consistent with his character; for he is a liar and the father of lies.

JOHN 8:44

In order to be effective on the battlefield, a soldier must be well trained and properly equipped. The warrior must have both a defensive stronghold and offensive weaponry. Combatants must know the enemy and be alert for surprise attacks. So it is in your spiritual battle with Satan. He is determined to destroy your faith by leading you into sin and discouragement, and he attacks you with blatant temptation and deceptive lies. The Bible is your field manual for fighting back. It trains you in the best weaponry and tactics for this very real and very dangerous spiritual warfare. Because Scripture is so essential for the Christian, Satan's first tactic in battle is to distort God's Word. If he can raise suspicion about the integrity of Scripture, he can get you to question God's will and intentions for you. Study the Bible so you know it well enough to recognize Satan's lies, which often come in the guise of cultural mores and worldviews. Satan's second tactic is to get you to rely on yourself instead of God. Satan will tempt you to rely on your own resources—on the tangible, measurable assets you can easily quantify. While it is wise to understand your resources, it is unwise to stake your ultimate victory on them. Prepare yourself with the resources God provides. Then rely on God's protection, not your own intellect or cleverness.

DIVINE PROMISE

PUT ON ALL OF GOD'S ARMOR SO THAT YOU WILL BE ABLE TO STAND FIRM AGAINST ALL STRATEGIES OF THE DEVIL.   *Ephesians 6:11*

Status

MY QUESTION *for* GOD

How can I use my status to glorify God?

A MOMENT *with* GOD

Choose a good reputation over great riches; being held in high esteem is better than silver or gold.

PROVERBS 22:1

Whoever wants to be first among you must be the slave of everyone else.   MARK 10:44

You call me "Teacher" and "Lord," and you are right,
because that's what I am. And since I, your Lord and
Teacher, have washed your feet, you ought to wash
each other's feet.   JOHN 13:13-14

Instead, [Jesus] gave up his divine privileges; he
took the humble position of a slave and was born as a
human being . . . in human form.   PHILIPPIANS 2:7

Status in and of itself is neither good nor bad. What
you do with your status is what counts. You can learn
the greatest lesson about status from Jesus himself.
The Bible tells us that as the Son of the all-powerful,
all-knowing, almighty God, Jesus was very rich and
powerful. Yet he gave up all of that to live on earth as
a human being, taking on the frailties of a human body
and then giving himself over to die a criminal's death so
the sins of the world would be paid for. Great status is
worth nothing unless used for great purposes. You can
use your status to build a good reputation that brings
honor to God's name, to serve and bless other people,
and to act on opportunities to point people to God. As
a leader, you can create divine moments in the lives of
others when you use your status to bless and serve for a
purpose greater than your own goals or plans.

DIVINE PROMISE

MANY WHO ARE THE GREATEST NOW WILL BE
LEAST IMPORTANT THEN, AND THOSE WHO
SEEM LEAST IMPORTANT NOW WILL BE THE
GREATEST THEN.   *Matthew 19:30*

Stewardship

MY QUESTION *for* GOD

How can I be a good steward?

A MOMENT *with* GOD

Cyrus directed Mithredath, the treasurer of Persia, to count these items and present them to Sheshbazzar, the leader of the exiles returning to Judah. This is a list of the items that were returned: gold basins . . . silver basins . . . silver incense burners.   EZRA 1:8-9

Here is the list of the Jewish exiles of the provinces who returned from their captivity.   EZRA 2:1

When they arrived at the Temple of the LORD in Jerusalem, some of the family leaders made voluntary offerings toward the rebuilding of God's Temple on its original site, and each leader gave as much as he could.   EZRA 2:68-69

Stewardship is managing what God has entrusted to you. Good managers seek to protect and to increase the assets given to their care. They know what and whom God has given them responsibility for. The Jewish exiles carefully recorded not only the temple treasures and donations, but also their human resources and even their animals! Take a few minutes to make a list of your stewardship responsibilities. Include the following: your financial resources and material possessions; your talents and time; and the people who are under your care, such as your family, the Sunday school class you teach, the senior citizen you visit at the nursing home, your Little League team, or the people you lead. Then pray and ask God how you can better manage these assets from him. The goal of stewardship is to make the best possible use of what God has entrusted to you in order to make the greatest possible impact on others. Ultimately good stewardship allows God's work to move forward as efficiently and effectively as possible.

DIVINE PROMISE

THE MASTER WAS FULL OF PRAISE. "WELL DONE, MY GOOD AND FAITHFUL SERVANT. YOU HAVE BEEN FAITHFUL IN HANDLING THIS SMALL AMOUNT, SO NOW I WILL GIVE YOU MANY MORE RESPONSIBILITIES. LET'S CELEBRATE TOGETHER!" *Matthew 25:21*

Strengths and Weaknesses

MY QUESTION *for* GOD

How can I maximize my strengths and minimize my weaknesses?

A MOMENT *with* GOD

I was given a thorn in my flesh, a messenger from Satan to torment me and keep me from becoming proud. Three different times I begged the Lord to take it away. Each time he said, "My grace is all you need. My power works best in weakness." So now I am glad to boast about my weaknesses, so that the power of Christ can work through me. That's why I take pleasure in my weaknesses, and in the insults, hardships, persecutions, and troubles that I suffer for Christ. For when I am weak, then I am strong.

2 CORINTHIANS 12:7-10

God gave these four young men an unusual aptitude for understanding every aspect of literature and wisdom.   DANIEL 1:17

I have filled him with the Spirit of God, giving him great wisdom, ability, and expertise in all kinds of crafts.   EXODUS 31:3

God has given us different gifts for doing certain things well. So if God has given you the ability to prophesy, speak out with as much faith as God has given you.   ROMANS 12:6

A petite, slender woman may appear at first glance to be physically weak, but actually she can run a marathon in less than three hours. A bodybuilder might appear to have great strength, but actually he demonstrates a weakness for drugs and alcohol. The Bible speaks about this tendency in our world for those things that appear to be strengths to actually be weaknesses, and vice versa. Sometimes what seems to be strong is very weak, and apparent weakness belies great strength. The key is not external appearances but internal character. As we grow in spiritual maturity, we learn to recognize and admit our weaknesses, and we learn to discover and exercise our strengths. Every person has both, so the presence of weaknesses need not trouble you. Work to maximize your strengths and improve in your areas of weakness. Also recognize the temptation to rely on your God-given strengths instead of the God who gives them, as well as the temptation to give in to your weaknesses while making the excuse that you don't have the strength to resist. As you learn your strengths and weaknesses, you discover how to use them both to grow closer to God.

DIVINE PROMISE

A SPIRITUAL GIFT IS GIVEN TO EACH OF US SO
WE CAN HELP EACH OTHER.   *1 Corinthians 12:7*

Stress

MY QUESTION *for* GOD

How can I reduce stress in my life?

A MOMENT *with* GOD

The Israelites did evil in the LORD's sight. . . . They abandoned the LORD. . . . He turned them over to their enemies all around, and they were no longer able to resist them. Every time Israel went out to battle, the LORD fought against them, causing them to be defeated, just as he had warned. And the people were in great distress.   JUDGES 2:11-12, 14-15

Certain actions have predictable consequences. If you try to stop a speeding car by stepping in front of it, you will get run over. The Bible talks about another kind of action that has an equally predictable consequence—sin. God's Word makes it clear that sin always hurts you because it separates you from God, your source of mercy and blessing, and puts you in the crosshairs of the enemy. Giving in to temptation will bring you great stress because it puts you right in the middle of the road, where evil hurtles toward you at high speed. Being run over by the consequences of sin causes great strain and enormous complications in your life. Of course, not all stress is caused by sinful actions; but the next time you are really feeling the stress, as the people of Israel were, your first response should be self-examination to check your heart and actions and see if there are areas of your life in which you are giving in to sin. Then get off the road of temptation before the consequences of sin run you over. Return to the Lord and ask for his help and mercy. God welcomes with open arms humble and repentant people, especially humble leaders.

DIVINE PROMISE

I HAVE TOLD YOU ALL THIS SO THAT YOU
MAY HAVE PEACE IN ME. HERE ON EARTH YOU
WILL HAVE MANY TRIALS AND SORROWS.
BUT TAKE HEART, BECAUSE I HAVE OVERCOME
THE WORLD. *John 16:33*

Success

MY QUESTION *for* GOD

Is it okay to try to be successful in this life?

A MOMENT *with* GOD

Work hard and become a leader; be lazy and become
a slave.   PROVERBS 12:24

Do you see any truly competent workers? They will
serve kings rather than working for ordinary people.
                                                  PROVERBS 22:29

Many godly character traits, such as hard work,
integrity, commitment, service, and planning, often
bring material success.

The LORD was with Joseph, so he succeeded in
everything he did as he served in the home of his
Egyptian master . . . giving him success in everything
he did.   GENESIS 39:2-3

The LORD blessed Job in the second half of his life
even more than in the beginning. For now he had
14,000 sheep, 6,000 camels, 1,000 teams of oxen,
and 1,000 female donkeys.   JOB 42:12

Throughout the Scriptures, God provides material
blessings for his people. While he does sometimes allow this for some people, God also urges them never

to forget the One who gave it to them. It is always a bad investment to pursue worldly success but sacrifice spiritual prosperity in the process.

The Lord said to Samuel, "Don't judge by his appearance or height, for I have rejected him. The Lord doesn't see things the way you see them. People judge by outward appearance, but the Lord looks at the heart."   1 Samuel 16:7

𝒢od's standards often differ greatly from our own. For a Christian, success is measured by faithfulness and fruitfulness, not revenue and profits. It is a spiritual assessment, not a numerical one. Too often success is measured in terms of appearances, finances, or other external qualities, but the Lord looks at your heart. God measures success not by prestige, possessions, or power, but by weighing your motives, your actions, and your devotion to him.

DIVINE PROMISE
WITH GOD'S HELP WE WILL DO
MIGHTY THINGS.   *Psalm 60:12*

Suffering

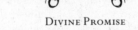

MY QUESTION *for* GOD

How do I help someone who is suffering?

A MOMENT *with* GOD

Going over to him, the Samaritan soothed his wounds
with olive oil and wine and bandaged them. Then he
put the man on his own donkey and took him to an
inn, where he took care of him.   LUKE 10:34

Share each other's burdens, and in this way obey the
law of Christ.   GALATIANS 6:2

If one part suffers, all the parts suffer with it, and if
one part is honored, all the parts are glad.

1 CORINTHIANS 12:26

Be happy with those who are happy, and weep with
those who weep.   ROMANS 12:15

Suffering is a universal experience. Some suffering
comes as a result of chance circumstances, such as a car
accident that maims someone or an illness that ravages
or even takes the life of a loved one. Some suffering
happens because of neglect, such as failure to prepare
for difficult times. Sometimes suffering comes because
you choose it, such as when you willingly take on enormous responsibilities in order to achieve a certain goal.
Other times suffering comes from sin, such as when
you deliberately go against God's commands and then
suffer the consequences. Whatever the source, at some
point everyone falls under the dark shadow of suffering. You won't always be able to explain it to those you
lead, but maybe the divine moment is realizing that you
don't have to explain it. We don't usually know why
suffering has come into the life of a certain person, and

one of the worst mistakes a leader can make is to lead in ignorance. Remind yourself of two important aspects of suffering—it hurts, but then it helps when it brings comfort to others. Suffering enables a person to comfort others, which becomes a divine moment for everyone. When you join in someone else's suffering, you choose to be wounded along with them. Woundedness may appear to weaken you, but it actually makes you stronger. When others are hurting, suffer along with them to bring them—and you—comfort and hope.

DIVINE PROMISE

ALL PRAISE TO GOD, THE FATHER OF OUR LORD JESUS CHRIST. GOD IS OUR MERCIFUL FATHER AND THE SOURCE OF ALL COMFORT. HE COMFORTS US IN ALL OUR TROUBLES SO THAT WE CAN COMFORT OTHERS. WHEN THEY ARE TROUBLED, WE WILL BE ABLE TO GIVE THEM THE SAME COMFORT GOD HAS GIVEN US.

2 Corinthians 1:3-4

Teaching

MY QUESTION *for* GOD

How can I be an effective spiritual teacher to those I lead?

A MOMENT *with* GOD

You yourself must be an example to them by doing good works of every kind. Let everything you do reflect the integrity and seriousness of your teaching.

TITUS 2:7

You must remain faithful to the things you have been taught. You know they are true, for you know you can trust those who taught you. You have been taught the holy Scriptures from childhood, and they have given you the wisdom to receive the salvation that comes by trusting in Christ Jesus.   2 TIMOTHY 3:14-15

Praise the LORD! How joyful are those who fear the LORD and delight in obeying his commands. Their children will be successful everywhere; an entire generation of godly people will be blessed. They themselves will be wealthy, and their good deeds will last forever.   PSALM 112:1-3

The godly walk with integrity; blessed are their children who follow them.   PROVERBS 20:7

I will teach you hidden lessons from our past— stories we have heard and known, stories our ancestors handed down to us. . . . We will tell the next generation about the glorious deeds of the LORD, about his power and his mighty wonders.

                                                       PSALM 78:2-4

A leader who is right with God has a much better chance of teaching others to become right with God. Others will follow the example you set. Throughout the Bible we see leaders passing on their own personal stories of faith. Here are some ways you can pass along a spiritual heritage to others:

- You can encourage them to experience a personal relationship with God, beginning with salvation through Jesus Christ.
- You can encourage them to live according to God's standards in the Bible, demonstrating by your own life how it gives joy and meaning to all you do.
- You can give them godly instruction based on Scripture.
- You can exemplify faith, obedience, and integrity. Those who love and respect you will follow in your footsteps.
- You can boldly tell your story of faith so others will see God's faithfulness to you.

If you do these things, you will effectively teach those around you and future generations about your faith. Many will follow in your footsteps, and God will be pleased with your efforts.

DIVINE CHALLENGE

BE AN EXAMPLE TO ALL BELIEVERS IN WHAT YOU SAY, IN THE WAY YOU LIVE, IN YOUR LOVE, YOUR FAITH, AND YOUR PURITY.   *1 Timothy 4:12*

Teamwork

MY QUESTION *for* GOD

It's just easier to do everything myself. Do I really need others to work with me?

A MOMENT *with* GOD

Eliashib the high priest and the other priests started to rebuild at the Sheep Gate. They dedicated it and set up its doors. . . . The Fish Gate was built by the sons of Hassenaah. They laid the beams, set up its doors, and installed its bolts and bars. Meremoth son of Uriah and grandson of Hakkoz repaired the next section of wall. . . . The Old City Gate was repaired by Joiada. . . . Next was Uzziel son of Harhaiah, a goldsmith by trade, who also worked on the wall. Beyond him was Hananiah, a manufacturer of perfumes. . . . Next to him, repairs were made by a group of Levites working under the supervision of Rehum son of Bani. Then came Hashabiah, the leader of half the district of Keilah, who supervised the building of the wall on behalf of his own district.

NEHEMIAH 3:1-8, 17

There are two important reasons for involving others in your ministry: The job is too big for one person, and everyone needs to buy in to the cause. Nehemiah knew he could not build the wall of Jerusalem by himself; he needed as many helpers as he could get. The church's mission and our mission as individual believers—making disciples of all nations (see Matthew 28:18-20)—is huge. We need as many people as possible if we are going to accomplish it. We also need to help others catch our vision. For Nehemiah, wall building was no longer seen as his pet project. Because he got the people involved, it became their passion. Likewise, a widespread sense of ownership of the work, whether a church's ministry or a business enterprise, is vital to an organization's success. As with a bank, the more people invest, the more interest they have.

DIVINE PROMISE

TWO PEOPLE ARE BETTER OFF THAN ONE, FOR THEY CAN HELP EACH OTHER SUCCEED. . . . THREE ARE EVEN BETTER, FOR A TRIPLE-BRAIDED CORD IS NOT EASILY BROKEN. *Ecclesiastes 4:9, 12*

Temptation

MY QUESTION *for* GOD

What makes temptation so hard to resist?

A MOMENT *with* GOD

She saw that the tree was beautiful and its fruit looked delicious . . . so she took some of the fruit and ate it.

GENESIS 3:6

*S*atan's favorite strategy is to make that which is sinful appear desirable and good. He also tries to make good

look evil. If he can make evil look good and good look
evil, then giving in to temptation appears right instead
of wrong. You must learn to recognize these moments,
when you are faced with a crucial choice between good
and bad. You must constantly be on guard against the
confusion Satan desires to create in you.

King Solomon loved many foreign women. . . . And
in fact, they did turn his heart away from the LORD.

                                              1 KINGS 11:1, 3

*O*ften temptation begins as seemingly harmless pleasure but soon gets out of control and progresses to full-
blown idolatry. In reality, the kind of pleasure that leads
to sin is never harmless. Before you give in to something
that seems innocent, look to God's Word for a reality
check. If Solomon had done this, he would have been
reminded that his pleasure was really sin. Perhaps he
would have been convicted and would have stopped sinning, preventing his life from becoming a wreck.

Then Jesus was led by the Spirit into the wilderness
to be tempted there by the devil. For forty days
and forty nights he fasted and became very hungry.
During that time the devil came and said to him, "If
you are the Son of God, tell these stones to become
loaves of bread." But Jesus told him, "No! The
Scriptures say, 'People do not live by bread alone, but
by every word that comes from the mouth of God.'"
Then the devil took him to the holy city, Jerusalem,
to the highest point of the Temple, and said, "If you

are the Son of God, jump off! For the Scriptures say,
'He will order his angels to protect you. And they
will hold you up with their hands so you won't even
hurt your foot on a stone.'" Jesus responded, "The
Scriptures also say, 'You must not test the LORD your
God.'" Next the devil took him to the peak of a very
high mountain and showed him all the kingdoms of
the world and their glory. "I will give it all to you,"
he said, "if you will kneel down and worship me."
"Get out of here, Satan," Jesus told him. "For the
Scriptures say, 'You must worship the LORD your
God and serve only him.'" Then the devil went away,
and angels came and took care of Jesus.   MATTHEW 4:1-11

*T*emptation often offers attractive short-term benefits, along with destructive, even deadly long-term
consequences. Temptation is often convincingly sea-
soned with partial truths. A leader must develop the
wisdom and discernment to know the difference between right and wrong, even when neither is black or
white at first glance.

DIVINE PROMISE

IF YOU THINK YOU ARE STANDING STRONG,
BE CAREFUL NOT TO FALL. THE TEMPTATIONS
IN YOUR LIFE ARE NO DIFFERENT FROM WHAT
OTHERS EXPERIENCE. AND GOD IS FAITHFUL.
HE WILL NOT ALLOW THE TEMPTATION TO BE
MORE THAN YOU CAN STAND. WHEN YOU ARE
TEMPTED, HE WILL SHOW YOU A WAY OUT SO
THAT YOU CAN ENDURE.   *1 Corinthians 10:12-13*

Testing

MY QUESTION *for* GOD

Does God really test my faith?

A MOMENT *with* GOD

Jeremiah, I have made you a tester of metals, that you may determine the quality of my people.   JEREMIAH 6:27

Dear brothers and sisters, when troubles come your way, consider it an opportunity for great joy. For you know that when your faith is tested, your endurance has a chance to grow. So let it grow, for when your endurance is fully developed, you will be perfect and complete, needing nothing.   JAMES 1:2-4

Remember how the LORD your God led you through the wilderness for these forty years, humbling you and testing you to prove your character, and to find out whether or not you would obey his commands.

DEUTERONOMY 8:2

Students are tested regularly to see if they are retaining and understanding the material they are learning. Auto consumers routinely take test drives to determine the quality of the vehicle they want to purchase. Companies invest vast sums in testing new products to guarantee they will perform as advertised. In the same way, our character and spiritual commitment are tested by the fires of hardship, persecution, and suffering. The Bible distinguishes between *temptation,* which Satan uses to lead us into sin, and *testing,* which God uses to purify us and move us toward spiritual growth and maturity. Out of testing comes a more committed faith. And out of a more committed faith comes a wiser and more committed leader. Just as commercial products are tested so that their performance can be strengthened, so also God tests your faith to strengthen you so you can accomplish all God wants you to do. When you feel like your faith is being tested, see it as a divine moment when God is working in your life to get your attention, to strengthen your relationship with him, and to help you be a greater influence on those you lead.

DIVINE PROMISE

THESE TRIALS WILL SHOW THAT YOUR FAITH
IS GENUINE.   *1 Peter 1:7*

Time

MY QUESTION *for* GOD

How can I find the time I need to do everything?

A MOMENT *with* GOD

Teach us to realize the brevity of life, so that we may grow in wisdom.   PSALM 90:12

Remember to observe the Sabbath day by keeping it holy. You have six days each week for your ordinary work, but the seventh day is a Sabbath day of rest dedicated to the LORD your God. . . . For in six days

the LORD made the heavens, the earth, the sea, and
everything in them; but on the seventh day he rested.
That is why the LORD blessed the Sabbath day and set
it apart as holy.   EXODUS 20:8-11

[Moses] told them, "This is what the LORD
commanded: Tomorrow will be a day of complete
rest, a holy Sabbath day set apart for the LORD. So
bake or boil as much as you want today, and set aside
what is left for tomorrow."   EXODUS 16:23

Be careful how you live. Don't live like fools,
but like those who are wise. Make the most of
every opportunity in these evil days. Don't act
thoughtlessly, but understand what the Lord wants
you to do. Don't be drunk with wine, because
that will ruin your life. Instead, be filled with the
Holy Spirit.   EPHESIANS 5:15-18

Time is a lot like the life of a battery—we rarely know
how much is left until it's gone. With time, though, we
cannot buy more or borrow more from someone else.
That is why time is so valuable. Yet we often live as
though it means so little. All of us would admit we waste
far too much time in doing things that aren't important
or significant. We let interruptions rule much of our day.
We know we should be more purposeful about how we
spend our time, but we're often unsure about how to
do that. The Bible is clear that how we use our precious
little time on earth will have an impact on our life in
heaven. We seem to live by the motto "So much to do,
so little time." But God does not ask you to do *everything*,

just everything he has called you to do, and he assures you that there is enough time for that. The more time you invest in discovering the purpose for which God created you and in living out that purpose with obedience and responsibility, the more meaningful and significant your time on earth will be. The best way to find the time you need is to devote time to God for worship and time to yourself for rest. Devoting time to God gives you spiritual refreshment and the opportunity to discover his priorities for you. Devoting time to rest gives you physical refreshment and the energy to do what you are called to do in the time you have.

DIVINE PROMISE

FOR EVERYTHING THERE IS A SEASON, A TIME FOR EVERY ACTIVITY UNDER HEAVEN. . . . GOD HAS MADE EVERYTHING BEAUTIFUL FOR ITS OWN TIME. HE HAS PLANTED ETERNITY IN THE HUMAN HEART.   *Ecclesiastes 3:1, 11*

Transition

MY QUESTION *for* GOD

I am transitioning into a leadership position. How do I get the best start?

A MOMENT *with* GOD

Moses my servant is dead. Therefore, the time has come for you to lead these people, the Israelites, across the Jordan River into the land I am giving them. . . . Be strong and very courageous. Be careful to obey all the instructions Moses gave you. Do not deviate from them, turning either to the right or to the left. Then you will be successful in everything you do. Study this Book of Instruction continually. Meditate on it day and night so you will be sure to obey everything written in it. Only then will you prosper and succeed in all you do. . . . Do not be afraid or discouraged. For the LORD your God is with you wherever you go.   JOSHUA 1:2, 7-9

When Moses died, Joshua became Israel's new leader. He probably felt a bit insecure; after all, he had pretty big sandals to fill. He may have wondered if he could lead the people as well as Moses had. The responsibilities must have felt overwhelming. God stepped in with encouragement and a remedy for insecurity: "Stay close to me, read my Word, be courageous, and remember that I am with you." And that's God's advice to you as well as you go through this transition.

DIVINE PROMISE
THOSE WHO FEAR THE LORD ARE SECURE.
Proverbs 14:26

Unity

MY QUESTION *for* GOD

What is the greatest threat to unity among believers?

A MOMENT *with* GOD

About this time some of the men and their wives
raised a cry of protest against their fellow Jews.
They were saying, "We have such large families. We
need more food to survive." Others said, "We have
mortgaged our fields, vineyards, and homes to get
food during the famine." And others said, "We have
had to borrow money on our fields and vineyards
to pay our taxes. We belong to the same family as
those who are wealthy, and our children are just like
theirs. Yet we must sell our children into slavery just
to get enough money to live. . . ." When I heard their
complaints, I was very angry. After thinking it over,
I spoke out against these nobles and officials. I told
them, " . . . What you are doing is not right! Should
you not walk in the fear of our God?"   NEHEMIAH 5:1-9

Satan's ultimate weapon is division. If he can get God's
people to fight with one another, he will have no worries
about God's kingdom advancing. Just when Nehemiah
had effectively addressed the problem of a military attack, a dispute broke out among the people about being
treated fairly. If Nehemiah had not handled the situation promptly and decisively, the city wall would have
remained unfinished and everyone would have been
vulnerable to attack. This happens too often with God's

people when they try to unite for a good cause. Sometimes the issues that divide Christians are tragically trivial. It is truly a divine moment if a leader can recognize when division among people is simple disagreement and when it is the result of spiritual warfare. You must prize unity and work tirelessly to maintain it, or else you and your people will become ineffective.

Divine Promise

HE MAKES THE WHOLE BODY FIT TOGETHER PERFECTLY. AS EACH PART DOES ITS OWN SPECIAL WORK, IT HELPS THE OTHER PARTS GROW, SO THAT THE WHOLE BODY IS HEALTHY AND GROWING AND FULL OF LOVE. *Ephesians 4:16*

Victory

My Question *for* God

How can I experience victory in my life?

A Moment *with* God

King Sihon declared war on us and mobilized his forces at Jahaz. But the Lord our God handed him over to us. . . . The Lord our God also helped us conquer Aroer . . . and the whole area as far as Gilead. . . . Next we turned and headed for the land of Bashan, where King Og and his entire army attacked us at Edrei. But the Lord told me, "Do not

be afraid of him, for I have given you victory over Og
and his entire army."   DEUTERONOMY 2:32-33, 36; 3:1-2

*W*ith God's help, the Israelites experienced victory
after victory as they marched toward the land God had
promised them. Your greatest victory has already been
won by Christ, when you received God's gift of salvation (see 1 John 5:4). But you need daily victory over
the strongholds of sin that threaten your ability to live
and lead effectively for God and be a victorious example to others. To experience victory in the Christian
life, commit yourself to vigorous spiritual training and
preparation (see Ephesians 6:10-18). This starts with
constant prayer and consistently reading and obeying
God's Word. In the passage above, we see that when
the people invited God to be part of their lives, and
when they consistently tried to obey him, they experienced victory. Too often leaders get so busy and
overwhelmed that they neglect God. He is no longer
their top priority. When you put God first, through
prayer and the study of his Word, you will experience
daily victory over sin and Satan's tactics to derail your
relationship with God and those you lead.

DIVINE PROMISE

STUDY THIS BOOK OF INSTRUCTION
CONTINUALLY. MEDITATE ON IT DAY AND
NIGHT SO YOU WILL BE SURE TO OBEY
EVERYTHING WRITTEN IN IT. ONLY THEN WILL
YOU PROSPER AND SUCCEED IN ALL YOU DO.

Joshua 1:8

Vision

MY QUESTION *for* GOD

How can I present a vision in a way that will mobilize people behind it?

A MOMENT *with* GOD

The city officials did not know I had been out [inspecting the walls] or what I was doing, for I had not yet said anything to anyone about my plans. I had not yet spoken to the . . . leaders . . . or anyone else in the administration. But now I said to them, "You know very well what trouble we are in. Jerusalem lies in ruins, and its gates have been destroyed by fire. Let us rebuild the wall of Jerusalem and end this disgrace!" Then I told them about how the gracious hand of God had been on me, and about my conversation with the king. They replied at once, "Yes, let's rebuild the wall!" So they began the good work.

NEHEMIAH 2:16-18

*A*im at nothing, and you'll hit it every time, the saying goes. A vision provides direction and motivation, and it is crucial in leadership. Research and timing are important to casting an effective vision. Nehemiah provides some pointers for how to present a vision: (1) help people see the significance of the vision and claim it as their own; (2) provide examples of how God has been and still is at work in your situation; and (3) outline a specific course of action, but don't get bogged down in minute details. Being able to cast a vision that

comes from God creates a divine moment not just for
you but for the entire group of people you lead.

DIVINE PROMISE

THE LORD IS AT THE HEAD OF THE COLUMN.
HE LEADS THEM WITH A SHOUT.   *Joel 2:11*

Vulnerability

MY QUESTION *for* GOD

When am I especially vulnerable in my work?

A MOMENT *with* GOD

Sanballat, Tobiah, Geshem the Arab, and the rest of
our enemies found out that I had finished rebuilding
the wall and that no gaps remained—though we had
not yet set up the doors in the gates. So Sanballat
and Geshem sent a message asking me to meet them.
. . . But I realized they were plotting to harm me,
so I replied by sending this message to them: "I
am engaged in a great work, so I can't come. Why
should I stop working to come and meet with you?"
Four times they sent the same message. . . . It said:
"There is a rumor among the surrounding nations,
and Geshem tells me it is true, that you and the Jews
are planning to rebel and that is why you are building
the wall. . . . You can be very sure that this report
will get back to the king. . . ." I replied, "There is no
truth in any part of your story. You are making up

the whole thing." They were just trying to intimidate us, imagining that they could discourage us and stop the work. So I continued the work with even greater determination.   NEHEMIAH 6:1-9

*W*hile you must be vigilant at all times, the first and final stages of an endeavor are especially vulnerable points. Jesus' greatest temptations came in the wilderness right as his ministry began (see Luke 4:1-13) and in the garden of Gethsemane just hours before he faced the cross (see Luke 22:39-46). At the point in Nehemiah's story described in the verses above, Jerusalem's walls were almost complete. If the people had taken the attitude, "We're as good as done, we can take it easy," they might have been caught by surprise by the fresh onslaught of false charges and intimidation from their enemies. If you relax too soon, it will result in misfortune. Start strong and push hard to the finish with energy and purpose to ensure that your work will withstand any pressures.

DIVINE PROMISE

LET'S NOT GET TIRED OF DOING WHAT IS
GOOD. AT JUST THE RIGHT TIME WE WILL REAP
A HARVEST OF BLESSING IF WE DON'T GIVE UP.

Galatians 6:9

Will of God

MY QUESTION *for* GOD

How do I know what God wants me to do?

A MOMENT *with* GOD

Coming to the borders of Mysia, they headed north for the province of Bithynia, but again the Spirit of Jesus did not allow them to go there. So instead, they went on through Mysia to the seaport of Troas. That night Paul had a vision: A man from Macedonia in northern Greece was standing there, pleading with him, "Come over to Macedonia and help us!" So we decided to leave for Macedonia at once, having concluded that God was calling us to preach the Good News there.

ACTS 16:7-10

God's will is both general and specific. God's will for all people is found in the Bible. It includes what God expects from everyone, such as obedience, service, worship, fellowship, and prayer. God's specific will is his plan for you as an individual. It may include your career, your marriage partner, or a unique task he wants you to accomplish. When you follow God's will for all people, you will be exactly where he wants you, and you will be fully prepared to step into his specific will when he calls you.

Wisdom

MY QUESTION *for* GOD

What are some of the characteristics of a wise person?

A MOMENT *with* GOD

Only fools say in their hearts, "There is no God."

PSALM 14:1

Fear of the LORD is the foundation of true
knowledge, but fools despise wisdom and discipline.

PROVERBS 1:7

A wise woman builds her home, but a foolish woman
tears it down with her own hands.   PROVERBS 14:1

Fools have no interest in understanding; they only
want to air their own opinions.   PROVERBS 18:2

To learn how to be wise, we can examine both wisdom and foolishness. The Bible describes fools as
having the following characteristics: they refuse to
acknowledge the existence of God; they make no attempt to develop wisdom or self-discipline; they are
entertained by making fun of what is good and moral;

they speak carelessly and thoughtlessly about others; and they think they are always right. Therefore, a wise person develops the opposite characteristics: they acknowledge a loving God who deeply cares about his people; they actively discipline themselves to pursue wisdom; they respect what is good and right and stand up against what is wrong; they find the good in others and encourage them; and they are humble enough to know they don't have all the answers.

Divine Promise

THE WISE ARE MIGHTIER THAN THE STRONG, AND THOSE WITH KNOWLEDGE GROW STRONGER AND STRONGER.   *Proverbs 24:5*

Work

My Question *for* God

How do I find meaning in my work?

A Moment *with* God

Make it your goal to live a quiet life, minding your own business and working with your hands, just as we instructed you before. Then people who are not Christians will respect the way you live, and you will not need to depend on others.   1 Thessalonians 4:11-12

Whatever you do or say, do it as a representative of
the Lord Jesus, giving thanks through him to God
the Father.   COLOSSIANS 3:17

You know that these hands of mine have worked to
supply my own needs and even the needs of those
who were with me. And I have been a constant
example of how you can help those in need by
working hard.   ACTS 20:34-35

Try to please them all the time, not just when they
are watching you. As slaves of Christ, do the will of
God with all your heart. Work with enthusiasm, as
though you were working for the Lord rather than
for people.   EPHESIANS 6:6-7

Work is part of God's plan for your life, and your work
matters to God. When you work diligently, you experience many benefits that you can pass on to others. At
its best, your work honors God and brings meaning
and joy to your life. You should emulate the qualities
found in God's work, such as excellence, concern for
the well-being of others, purpose, beauty, and service.
When you have the perspective that you are actually
working for God, you can focus less on the task at hand
and more on your motives—to help people know God.
The excitement and interest that come from having this
perspective are not primarily from the work but from
the One for whom you work. God promises these re-
wards for faithful work, regardless of the job: You are a
more credible witness to nonbelievers, and your needs
are met without having to depend on others financially.

There is immense dignity in all honest human labor, for your work is an opportunity to serve God and others. Christians are needed in all kinds of vocations. Whatever your job, remember that God has placed you there for a reason. Do your work to the best of your ability as a service to God and others until God opens a door of opportunity for you to move on.

DIVINE PROMISE

WORK WILLINGLY AT WHATEVER YOU DO, AS THOUGH YOU WERE WORKING FOR THE LORD RATHER THAN FOR PEOPLE. REMEMBER THAT THE LORD WILL GIVE YOU AN INHERITANCE AS YOUR REWARD, AND THAT THE MASTER YOU ARE SERVING IS CHRIST. *Colossians 3:23-24*

Worship

MY QUESTION *for* GOD

Why is it hard to worship?

A MOMENT *with* GOD

Oh, how great are God's riches and wisdom and knowledge! How impossible it is for us to understand his decisions and his ways! For who can know the LORD's thoughts? Who knows enough to give him advice? And who has given him so much that he needs to pay it back? For everything comes from him and exists by his power and is intended for his glory. All glory to him forever! Amen. ROMANS 11:33-36

This is what the LORD says: "Heaven is my throne, and the earth is my footstool. Could you build me a temple as good as that? Could you build me such a resting place? My hands have made both heaven and earth; they and everything in them are mine. I, the LORD, have spoken! I will bless those who have humble and contrite hearts, who tremble at my word."   ISAIAH 66:1-2

It has been said that worship is offering extravagant devotion to someone or something. By that definition, every human being worships something. What or who we worship defines the value and purpose of our lives. When we worship God with extravagant devotion, we acknowledge his power and glory, and we experience his presence through the Holy Spirit. Our worship defines and expresses our relationship to God.

It may be hard for leaders to worship because leaders are used to calling the shots, being in charge, having others "worship" them, in the sense that others give them their attention and devotion. As leaders get used to telling others what to do, it becomes more difficult for them to let God tell them what to do. But never forget that one of the great purposes of worship is to help you see the holiness of God so you can better understand the sinfulness in your own heart. Only then can you draw closer to God, as you confess your sinfulness and experience his grace and forgiveness. Worship, then, is recognizing who God is, and who you are in relation to him. You realize how great is the gulf between you and God, you understand how unworthy you are, and you know how important it is to have your heart prepared to fellowship with him. Take a divine moment and praise God whenever you see his wisdom, power, direction, care, and love in your life. Then worship will become a way of life.

DIVINE PROMISE

THEREFORE, GOD ELEVATED HIM TO THE PLACE OF HIGHEST HONOR AND GAVE HIM THE NAME ABOVE ALL OTHER NAMES, THAT AT THE NAME OF JESUS EVERY KNEE SHOULD BOW, IN HEAVEN AND ON EARTH AND UNDER THE EARTH, AND EVERY TONGUE CONFESS THAT JESUS CHRIST IS LORD, TO THE GLORY OF GOD THE FATHER.

Philippians 2:9-11

Wrestling with God

MY QUESTION *for* GOD

What does it mean to wrestle with God?

A MOMENT *with* GOD

During the night Jacob got up and . . . crossed the Jabbok River. . . . A man came and wrestled with him until the dawn began to break. When the man saw that he would not win the match, he touched Jacob's hip and wrenched it out of its socket. Then the man said, "Let me go, for the dawn is breaking!" But Jacob said, "I will not let you go unless you bless me." "What is your name?" the man asked. He replied, "Jacob." "Your name will no longer be Jacob," the man told him.

"From now on you will be called Israel, because you have fought with God and with men and have won." . . . Jacob named the place Peniel (which means "face of God"), for he said, "I have seen God face to face, yet my life has been spared."   Genesis 32:22-30

It was time for Jacob's life to be radically changed. Jacob the deceiver had to become Israel the defender of God. Jacob, the shrewd negotiator who knew how to get ahead in life, had to learn to see from a heavenly perspective. The name Israel literally means "God prevails." But the angel turned the meaning around to mean "You have prevailed (or struggled) with God." In other words, Jacob could now become victorious in life because he finally recognized he could not overcome without the power and authority of God. When Jacob received this new name after his encounter with God, it was a turning point, a divine moment, in his life. From then on his life had to take a new direction if he was to be a worthy leader of the people of God. In what areas of your life are you wrestling with God? In what areas do you think you have it all figured out? In what areas do you rarely, if ever, ask God for help? It is in those areas especially that you must let God's power and authority overcome you. Then be prepared to go in new directions and live a life worthy of a child of God.

Divine Promise

I CAN DO EVERYTHING THROUGH CHRIST, WHO GIVES ME STRENGTH. *Philippians 4:13*

Index

DIVINE
MOMENTS
Books